Cites& Sources

An APA Documentation Guide

Fourth Edition

Jane Haig
Georgian College

Vicki MacMillan
Georgian College

Gail Raikes
Georgian College

NELSON / EDUCATION

NELSON / EDUCATION

Cites & Sources: An APA Documentation Guide, Fourth Edition

by Jane Haig, Vicki MacMillan, and Gail Raikes

Vice President, Editorial Higher Education:
Anne Williams

Executive Editor:
Laura Macleod

Executive Marketing Manager:
Amanda Henry

Developmental Editor:
Theresa Fitzgerald

Permissions Coordinator:
Yvonne Liburd

Content Production Manager:
Lila Campbell

Copy Editor/Proofreader:
Lila Campbell

Senior Production Coordinator:
Ferial Suleman

Design Director:
Ken Phipps

Managing Designer:
Franca Amore

Interior Design:
Carianne Sherriff and Heather Holm

Cover Design:
Dave Murphy

Cover and Frontispiece Image:
Ben Bloom/Getty Images

Compositor:
Carianne Sherriff

Printer:
RR Donnelley

Library and Archives Canada Cataloguing in Publication Data

Haig, Jane
Cites & sources : an APA documentation guide / Jane Haig, Vicki MacMillan, Gail Raikes. — 4th ed.

Includes bibliographical references and index.

ISBN 978-0-17-650852-4

1. Bibliographical citations—Handbooks, manuals, etc.
2. Report writing—Handbooks, manuals, etc. I. MacMillan, Vicki II. Raikes, Gail III. Title. IV. Title: Cites and sources.

PN171.F56H36 2013
808.02'7   C2012-906920-5

ISBN-13: 978-0-17-650852-4
ISBN-10: 0-17-650852-X

Table of Contents

Acknowledgements

This fourth edition of *Cites & Sources* is updated to reflect ongoing changes in APA formatting, particularly in electronic formats. Included in this edition are scenarios dealing with plagiarism; new examples of correct quoting and paraphrasing; a new research report on a timely topic, the local food movement in Canada; and revised information on citing sources and preparing reference entries. In addition, Sections 4 and 6 contain almost all new entries, the majority of which are Canadian examples.

We acknowledge with gratitude the contribution of Colleen O'Brien, a graduate of Laurentian University, for permission to use her essay, "We'll Rant and We'll Roar Like True Newfoundlanders: Newfoundland Nationalism." As always, we acknowledge and appreciate the comments and suggestions of colleagues, students, and friends in the preparation of this new edition.

In particular, we thank Heather Holm, our designer and photographer for the text. We appreciate her insightful guidance on incorporating design features that make the text current and accessible for students and a viable "teaching tool" for the classroom. The photographs with their accompanying quotations add visual interest and are in keeping with a "green" theme for this text. We believe that raising awareness of the fragility of our planet is everyone's responsibility and this is one small measure on our part to do so.

Introduction to APA

The American Psychological Association (APA) style of documentation is commonly recognized as a standard documentation style for colleges, universities, and businesses.

A consistent style of documentation in research papers

- Provides uniformity to the paper
- Allows readers to give full attention to content
- Presents ideas in a form and style accepted by and familiar to readers

This fourth edition is updated to reflect changes in the sixth edition (2010) of the *Publication Manual of the American Psychological Association*, particularly in referencing electronic sources.

1 Getting Started

"We are so small, and the great aerial ocean so vast, that it seems hardly credible that we could do anything to affect its equilibrium. Indeed, for most of the past century humans have held to the belief that climate is largely stable, and that the flea on the elephant's buttock that is humanity can have no effect. Yet if we were to imagine Earth as an onion, our atmosphere would be no thicker than its outermost parchment skin."

Tim Flannery, 2005

Flannery, T. (2005). *The weather makers.* Toronto, Canada: HarperCollins.

Photo © Heather Holm

Selecting a Research Topic

Once you have selected a topic for research, you need to consult many sources, including books, academic journals, magazines, newspapers, and online information.

PLAGIARISM

To avoid plagiarism, you must document all ideas and direct quotations in your paper using APA style. See **Plagiarism,** p. 7.

Proper documentation requires that you

1 Acknowledge source references within your paper. See **Section 3: Citing Sources**.

2 List your sources at the end of your paper. See **Section 6: References List Entries**.

Documentation in the Essay

NEWFOUNDLAND NATIONALISM   5
    While the media might have weakened Newfoundlanders and their identity in the early 20th century, it has done much for the cultural nationalism that is prevalent today. As Millard, Riegel, and Wright (2002) argued, "The relative decline of state institutions as transmitters of cultures and identity in favour of commodified expressions of these goods may be affecting the tone and content of Canadian Nationalism" (p. 12). So, too, does the commodified expression of Newfoundland's pop culture transmit her identity to the rest of Canada and the world.

References List Entry

NEWFOUNDLAND NATIONALISM   9
            References
Millard, G., Riegel, S., & Wright, J. (2002). Here's where we get Canadian: English-Canadian nationalism and pop culture. *The American Review of Canadian Studies, 32*(1), 11–34. http://dx.doi.org /10.1080/02722010209481654
Overton, J. (1988). A Newfoundland culture? *Journal of Canadian Studies, 23*(1), 2–22.
Story, G. M., Kirwin, W. J., & Widdowson, J. D. (Eds.). (1999). *Dictionary of Newfoundland English* (2nd ed.). Retrieved from http://www.heritage .nf.ca/dictionary

Research

Your research begins with evaluating print and electronic resources to determine the most useful sources of information for your report or paper.

Consider the following criteria:

ACCURACY

Is the information contained in the document both **relevant** and **accurate**?

Check the publisher/producer for **credibility**.

For example:

A government publication such as *Statistics Canada* can be considered **reliable**.

A website developed by someone interested in promoting a particular point of view or product using **questionable** statistics may not be reliable.

CONTENT

Is there enough **detailed** information on the topic?

Is the information at an **appropriate level** for the topic?

CURRENCY

Is the information **up-to-date** and/or **relevant**?

If the information is from a website, when was it last **updated**?

AUTHORITY

Who is **responsible** for the information?

Is the producer/publisher the same as the author?

Are **credentials** listed?

Is there an advertiser/sponsor relationship?

Is the resource wiki-based, allowing anyone to contribute?

Note: While Wikipedia may be a good place to start your research, it is generally **NOT acceptable as an academic reference** due to its questionable reliability.

OBJECTIVITY

Is the information **biased**?

Is the producer actually an advertiser **promoting** a product?

If the resource is a website, check the domain name for clues to ownership.

Taking Notes

Research involves taking notes in which you summarize, paraphrase, and directly quote information from your reference sources.

Be sure to include all of the information necessary to correctly document your sources when it comes time to write your paper.

While taking notes, clearly distinguish between paraphrased material and direct quotations, and include the following:

APA requires **BOTH** an **in-text citation** and a **References list entry** for each research source used in your report or paper.

You can't have one without the other!

NOTES

1 Title of Material Used

2 Author's Name

3 Pages Consulted

4 Publication Data: Date, Place, and Publisher

5 Access Information for Electronic Materials

6 DOI

Plagiarism

Plagiarism is the presentation of someone else's words or ideas as your own — and is a **serious academic offence**. Whether you are quoting or putting an idea or fact into your own words, you must cite your source. See *Section 3: Citing Sources*.

PLAGIARISM

Plagiarism will not be an issue or a temptation if you have a detailed plan in place to write your paper and you ensure your own ideas form the basis for your thesis (central argument).

For your planning, take into account the following:

1   complexity of the topic
2   research required for the topic
3   time available to complete the paper

PENALTIES!

Penalties for plagiarism, even if unintentional, may range from a **zero** on the paper to **expulsion** from the institution. Protect yourself by scrupulously documenting all your sources.

AVOIDING PLAGIARISM

You can avoid plagiarism and its subsequent penalties by following these guidelines for your paper:

1   **Keep records** of all the sources you consult during your research and note-taking. See *Taking Notes* on the previous page.
2   Use your research notes to support, not replace, your own ideas.
3   Prepare a draft of the References list as you work.
4   Check to ensure all your **sources are documented** before submitting your paper.
5   Never copy and paste from electronic sources without documentation.
6   Never submit a paper purchased or copied electronically from a writing service.
7   Never submit a copy of someone else's paper as your own.

AVOIDING PLAGIARISM: SCENARIOS

The Internet makes available a full range of research material. Copying and pasting material from online sources directly into your paper is plagiarism and is easily detectable with plagiarism software used by many colleges and universities. A defence that you didn't intend to plagiarize or that you forgot to document sources does not excuse the offence. Whether plagiarism is intentional or unintentional, students are subject to their college's or university's penalties for plagiarism.

If you are having difficulty with a paper, access the writing services, tutoring services, and counselling services available at your college. Some colleges also have "buddies" or mentors for new students.

The following scenarios illustrate situations students may encounter:

SCENARIO 1

"A" has been working on her paper for her biology class for several weeks; she's gathered lots of material, mostly from online resources, that she's copied and pasted into a file. It will be easy, she thinks, to find the material again and make notes of the information required for in-text citations and reference entries. She finds, however, in writing her paper that she can't find the information for an online source from which she wants to quote several lines. The quote is just perfect for her paper. What to do? Use the material without quotation marks and risk plagiarism? A "few" lines shouldn't matter, should it? If only she had taken the time to copy the link to the source when she was doing her research. She submits her paper without the in-text citation or reference entry. Her biology professor, very familiar with this topic and source, recognizes the quotation immediately. "A" is charged with plagiarism and subject to the penalties of her college.

SCENARIO 2

"B" is dealing with a difficult and complicated topic and he is having trouble formulating a thesis. He's read so much he isn't sure what his own ideas are! Now he has to come up with a thesis, a point of view that he can support. What to do? He starts by writing points that he finds important and interesting about his topic. From those points he realizes he has developed a point of view on his subject. Choosing three main ideas that support his point of view, he starts to write an outline. From the outline, his thesis or point of view is clarified and his introduction written. In the paper, his extensive research supports his thesis and is documented with in-text citations and a References page. It took a lot of time to research and write the paper, but the effort is worth it as he has learned a lot about the subject and discovered that he has ideas of his own.

SCENARIO 3

"C" is an organized person. As she writes her paper and inserts in-text citations, she completes the reference entries for the sources in a draft online file of the References page. Putting the finishing touches on her paper the day before the due date, she has only to consult the online file of her sources and check the accuracy of the in-text citations and reference entries. Then she checks that the reference entries are listed in alphabetical order by author and all required parts of the entry are there. She knows that if there is a reference entry, there must be an in-text citation and vice versa.

SCENARIO 4

For "D", English is a second language and he has been struggling not only with the language but also with the cultural differences in his new surroundings, trying to adapt to this country's ways and to make new friends at his college. Exhausted from his long overseas trip to his new country, he did not attend his college's orientation and workshops on documentation and plagiarism and is not aware that his college has a writing service he can access for help with papers. However, his electronic translator has been a big help as he struggles to understand the complexity of the language in his textbooks. When he is assigned a paper in his economics class, he despairs and texts his brother back home who is studying economics at university and asks for help. His brother e-mails him a copy of one of his papers on the topic assigned and "D" downloads it to his electronic translator for an English translation. Trying to fit the requirements of his own assignment, "D" makes a few changes to the paper, unaware he has committed plagiarism. As soon as his economics professor. starts to grade "D's" paper, she spots inconsistencies in language, both in level and use, research at a higher level than required for the topic, off-topic information and conclusions, and a different system of documentation than required. "D" is called in to meet with his professor.

EXAMPLES OF PLAGIARIZED AND CORRECTLY DOCUMENTED TEXT

The original text was taken from the February, 2012 article, "In the Company of Strangers," in *Report on Business* magazine. The article is a research source in a student paper on changes in the workplace.

ORIGINAL TEXT

"With fewer traditional openings on the market, and job security scarce, more people are willing to strike out on their own with a business idea or accept project work, especially if they can share the costs of office resources. Ever-improving mobile and cloud computing technology continues to make fixed addresses less relevant. At the same time, more businesses are having their employees work remotely either part-time or full-time, while the ranks of the self-employed (some 2.6 million in Canada, as of November, 2011) continue to grow" (MacLellan, 2012, p. 16).

MacLellan, L. (2012, February). In the company of strangers. *Report on Business*, *28*(7), 14–16.

PLAGIARIZED: SLIGHT CHANGES IN WORDING

Coworking, the concept of sharing workspace with compatible people, either self-employed or with an employer, is a growing practice in the workplace. With not many traditional openings on the market, and little job security, people are willing to strike out on their own with a business idea. Improved mobile and cloud computing technology makes fixed addresses not as important. Coworking is also very much understood by businesses who have both full- and part-time employees working off-site. Not only does coworking provide a business environment, it also can spark creativity among ...

CORRECTLY DOCUMENTED:
Direct Quotation

Coworking, the concept of sharing workspace with compatible people, either self-employed or with a different employer, is expanding in the workplace. A recent article in *Report on Business* noted some of the reasons for the growth in coworking such as "ever-improving mobile and cloud computing technology" that make "fixed addresses less relevant" and especially attractive and beneficial to the self-employed (MacLellan, 2012, p. 16). The spinoffs to coworking are many ...

CORRECTLY DOCUMENTED:
Direct Quotation

Coworking, the concept of sharing workspace with compatible people, either self-employed or with a different employer, is expanding in the workplace. The number of self-employed Canadian workers, as reported in an article by Lila MacLellan in *Report on Business* (2012), has increased to "some 2.6 million in Canada as of November, 2011" (p. 16), largely contributing to the growth of shared space. Not only do the self-employed have access to the latest technology in their space, they also have the opportunity to interact with other workers ...

CORRECTLY DOCUMENTED:
Paraphrased

Coworking, the concept of sharing workspace with compatible people, either self-employed or with a different employer, is a growing practice in the workplace. According to an article in the February, 2012 *Report on Business*, more self-employed and distance workers have contributed to the popularity of shared space for work (MacLellan, p. 16). Another advantage to coworking is the opportunity to interact with other workers ...

CORRECTLY DOCUMENTED:
Paraphrased

Coworking, the concept of sharing workspace with compatible people, either self-employed or with a different employer, is a growing practice. A current article noted that shared space provides interaction with others and technology to communicate with mobile and computer devices, making this practice a viable alternative to the traditional workplace (MacLellan, 2012, p. 16). The interaction among those sharing workspace can contribute to productivity ...

2 Formatting Your Paper

"I was surprised at the number and variety of brilliantly-coloured butterflies; they were all of small size, and started forth at every step I took, from the low bushes which bordered the road."

Henry Walter Bates, 1873

Bates, H. W. (2005). *The naturalist on the river Amazons.* Boston, MA: Adamant Media.
   (Original work published 1873)

Photo © Heather Holm

Formatting Your Paper

A successful research essay or report must be professionally formatted and presented. First impressions count!

This section presents a **sample title/cover page, essay and report models, and References page formatted** according to the following APA guidelines. Consult with your instructor or refer to other documentation manuals for more detailed information on formatting and organizing specific kinds of reports.

MATERIALS AND TYPEFACE

Use good-quality 8 1/2" × 11" white paper. Select **Times New Roman, 12 point**, as the preferred font. All documents should be word-processed and printed using a high-quality printer.

TITLE/COVER PAGE

Begin your paper with a **title/cover page**. Place a **running head** in full caps one inch from the top and flush with the left margin. On the same line, indented five spaces from the right margin, place the **page number**. Centre and double-space the text in the upper half of the page. Use **mixed case letters** to type the following: the **title** of your paper, your name, the name and **section** of your course, your **instructor's name**, and the **date**.

PAGE NUMBERS AND RUNNING HEADS

In full caps, type a running head, an abbreviation of the title, flush with the left margin of every page including the title/cover page. The running head has a maximum of 50 characters, including letters, spaces, and punctuation. Beginning with the title/cover page, number all pages including tables, appendices, and the References page.

MARGINS, SPACING, AND INDENTATION

Use **one-inch margins** (2.54 cm) on all sides of the page (top, bottom, right, and left). **Double-space** the entire paper, and **indent the first line** of each paragraph one tab. **Tab indent** each line of long quotations (longer than forty words) and double-space the lines of the quotation.

HEADINGS

Headings help to organize the presentation of your research and are required for most reports. Because it is assumed that your first paragraph is the introduction, do not use "Introduction" as a heading. Centre and bold **first-level headings** (major divisions) and use mixed case letters. Left justify and bold **second-level headings** and use mixed case. Bold **third-level headings** and indent one tab from the left margin. Capitalize the first word only, place a period at the end of the heading, and begin the paragraph immediately following. For documents requiring more than three levels of headings, refer to the APA manual.

ABSTRACT/SUMMARY

An abstract or summary provides an **overview** of your paper. It should include your **central idea**, **key points**, and any **implications** or **applications** discussed in your paper. Consult your instructor for more specific details and requirements.

An abstract or summary **immediately follows** the title/cover page. Type "Abstract" or "Summary" as the main heading, **centred** and at the top of the page. An abstract or summary does not usually exceed one page.

APPENDIX

An appendix is located at the **end** of a report following the **References list** and contains additional information referred to in the report.

For example:

You might want to include a **copy of a survey** form (questionnaire or interview questions) that you used to collect data for your report. Each appendix is labelled **Appendix A**, **B**, **C**, and so on, according to the order it is referred to in the report.

SUPPLEMENTARY MATERIAL

Specific kinds of reports may require **additional** supplementary materials — such as an **executive summary**, a **memo** or **letter of transmittal**, **interview transcripts**, and so on.

Ask your instructor or consult your course textbook for how to arrange and place these supplementary materials.

VISUALS

Reports often include visuals to clarify and summarize research findings. Visuals are used to **complement** rather than to duplicate text.

Tables, for example, present exact numerical data arranged in columns and rows.

Figures include graphs, charts, maps, illustrations, drawings, and photographs.

Tables and figures allow readers to see the overall **pattern of results**, eliminating the need for lengthy discussion.

DO NOT include any visuals that you do not clearly introduce and explain in your text.

Ask your instructor for specific assignment guidelines on placing, labelling, and numbering the pages of your visuals.

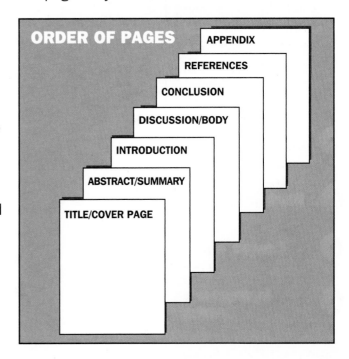

ORDER OF PAGES

APPENDIX
REFERENCES
CONCLUSION
DISCUSSION/BODY
INTRODUCTION
ABSTRACT/SUMMARY
TITLE/COVER PAGE

Sample Title/Cover Page

Centre information in upper half of page and **double-space**

Indent **page number** five spaces from right margin; on same line, include "Running head:" in mixed case, flush left, followed by a shortened version of the title in full caps (a maximum of 50 characters)

A

B **Title** in **mixed case**

C **Student's name**

D **Course name**

E **Instructor's name**

F **Date**

A Running head: NEWFOUNDLAND NATIONALISM   1

B We'll Rant and We'll Roar Like True Newfoundlanders:

Newfoundland Nationalism

C Colleen O'Brien

D Political Science – UPO1107-01

E Professor Geoff Booth

F Friday, March 19, 2007

Sample Essay

G NEWFOUNDLAND NATIONALISM   2

L

H We'll Rant and We'll Roar Like True Newfoundlanders:

I Newfoundland Nationalism

J A feeling of pride wells to the surface whenever a Newfoundlander **K** speaks of home. Home is, of course, the rugged, craggy island of rock in the North Atlantic Ocean. But it is more than geography. Even if he or she has lived on the mainland of Canada most of his or her adult life, a Newfoundlander is just that: Newfoundlander first, Canadian second. More than just a regional identity, Newfoundlanders have a passionate sense of commonality that cannot be easily explained in words or understood by those who are not part of it. This sense of community has always fostered nationalism in Newfoundland, but there seems to be a new movement of nationalism sweeping its shores: it is a neo-nationalism led not by politicians, but by a new generation of islanders who are proud of their heritage and culture. In Hollywood movies, award-winning literature, popular music, and international media, Newfoundland culture is a hot commodity.

J Cultural nationalism is not a new phenomenon in Canadian politics. The rights revolution, as defined by Michael Ignatieff, is one of the many offspring born of a marital diversity in a political community known for its tolerance. The difficulty with this fractured version of Canadian politics is where we draw the line. Cultural nationalism is one thing, but to take that one step further in the form of civic nationalism, as the Quebec separatist movement has tried to do, is a maple leaf of a whole different colour. Canadian Aboriginals are identified and recognized as a distinct society, with special political provisions afforded them by law. Quebec is still fighting for preferential treatment by the federal government. In Newfoundland, the movement toward both civic nationalism and distinct status is gathering momentum and is the source of potential socioeconomic implications for the entire country of Canada.

L

Colleen O'Brien Essay ©

G Include a **running head** and **page number** on every page

H **Centre** the **title** and use **mixed case**

I **Double-space** between the **title** and the **first line** and all text

J **Tab** indent the first line of each paragraph

K Use Times New Roman or a similar **font** and **12 point type**

L Leave one-inch **margins** (top, bottom, right, and left)

Sample Report

Use Times New Roman or similar **font** and 12 point type	
A **Centre** the **title** and use mixed case	
B **Double-space** between the title and the first line and all text	

THE LOCAL FOOD MOVEMENT IN CANADA   2

A   The Local Food Movement in Canada

B   While pastoral barnyard scenes featured on the packaging of dairy, vegetable, and meat products regularly purchased from our supermarkets suggest reassuring images of an agrarian Canada, these foods are largely produced by an industrialized food system that belies the "pastoral fantasy" we associate with healthy living and eating. In fact, "the way we eat now has changed more over the last 50 years than in the previous 10,000" (Kenner & Perlstein, 2008).

Despite the appearance of a variety of product choices in our supermarkets, a small number of large corporations — Heinz, Kellogg, Kraft, Nestle, Cadbury — dominate food production and distribution, based on an industrial model that has failed to address a growing global food crisis in which close to 1 billion of the world's 6 billion people suffer from hunger and starvation. Although the American Food and Agriculture Organization (FAO) estimates that there is currently enough food to feed the world's population, by the year 2030 "it is anticipated that there will need to be an increase in food production of between 50 and 100 per cent over current levels if the world is to feed its people" (Lawrence, Lyons, & Wallington, 2010, p. 1). In Canada, 14.7 percent of people "live in food-insecure households (Pegg, 2007) and 7 percent are chronically hungry" (Miller, 2008, p. 11).

In addition to failing to address this food crisis, contemporary food systems have led to a rapid decline in family farming, a depletion of energy reserves as a result of the distance "from farm to fork" or "foodmiles," as well as environmental costs that include "stream and river pollution caused by toxic chemicals, the genetic pollution and biodiversity losses associated with the expansion of genetically modified (GM) crops, and the atmospheric impact of greenhouse gases (largely methane) produced by livestock" (Lawrence, Lyons, & Wallington, 2010, p. 7).

E

THE LOCAL FOOD MOVEMENT IN CANADA   3 **D**

    Several recent studies (Miller, 2008; Smithers, Lamarche, & Joseph, 2008; Wittman, Desmarais, & Wiebe, 2010) have suggested that the growing public support in Canada of local food production is part of a broader political and social movement for changes in international policies to address a global agri-food crisis. It is important to understand the current situation and data both nationally and locally. To that end, the purpose of this report is to provide an overview of the local food movement in Canada and current studies of the practice and impact of local food initiatives.

C **Discussion**

    By focusing concerns on the social, economic, and environmental costs of industrialized food production and "factory farms," local food movements over the past decade have initiated transformational possibilities in the way we produce and consume our daily bread. The relationship between food **E** and social change has become increasingly evident in recent studies and **E** arguments for "edible action," or food activism (Miller, 2008).

    In Canada, the local food movement, or "locavore," involves a cross-section of activists. They range from farmers and consumers to academic and government research and policy makers, non-governmental organizations such as Toronto's FoodShare, "a non-profit agency working to improve access to affordable and healthy food from field to table" ("What We Do," 2012), and governmental agencies such as Toronto's Food Policy Council (TFPC) founded in 1990 as a subcommittee of the city's Board of Health (Wekerle, 2004, p. 382). ... [Text continues in full report]

F Consumer Power

    Increasing consumer awareness of the need for healthy, cost-effective, and environmentally sustainable food production has, in part, as Morrison, Nelson, and Ostry (2011) argued, grown out of the "emergence of periodic food safety crises [that] have alarmed the public" such as "mad cow" disease, the contamination of milk in China, and an outbreak of Listeriosis at a Maple Leaf Foods' Canadian processing plant (p. 491). Moreover, it is

E

C Centre and bold **first-level headings**; use mixed case

D Place the **page number** and **running head** on the same line

E Leave **one-inch margins** (top, bottom, right, and left)

F Left justify and bold **second-level headings**; use mixed case

G Include a **running head** and **page number** on every page

H **Tab indent** the first line of each paragraph

THE LOCAL FOOD MOVEMENT IN CANADA   4 **G**

estimated that in the United States one in three children born after 2000 will contract early onset diabetes (Kenner & Pearlstein, 2008). Over the past twenty years, consumer demand for knowledge of just what we are eating has led to more comprehensive product labeling (e.g., "Nutritional Facts"), organic food sections in major grocery chains, increased support of farmers' markets, and a general concern for healthy food consumption. In addition, organic farm operations in Canada increased from 0.9% in 2001 to 1.8% in 2011 according to the recent Census of Agriculture (Statistics Canada, 2012, para. 21).

H More recently, however, and fuelled by a greater awareness of the environmental, social, and economic costs of our current industrialized farming system, advocates for local food initiatives have begun to change more radically the relationship between food and daily community living. The movement towards consuming locally-produced foods received even greater attention and popularity with the publication of *The 100-Mile Diet: A Year of Local Eating* (2007). In this Canadian national bestseller, writers Smith and MacKinnon documented their year-long adventure with eating only food grown and produced within a 100-mile radius of their apartment in Vancouver…. [Text continues in full report]

The considerable efforts of food activists and the growing demand by consumers for locally produced foods and alternatives to purchasing from corporate grocery chains — seven of which control 70% of the Canadian market (Miller, 2008, p. 54) — have initiated major changes in the marketing, availability, and affordability of local, organic, and more environmentally sustainable foods. The Ontario government's Foodland Ontario, for example, established in 1977 as a consumer promotion program for Ontario food, now consists of three program components: brand services, retail services, and grower services. According to their website, the main objective of Foodland Ontario is to maintain an 80% consumer intent to buy Ontario produced foods. Foodland Ontario now provides product labelling

THE LOCAL FOOD MOVEMENT IN CANADA   5

and extensive media and public relations that include television commercials with the theme lines of "Good things grow in Ontario" and, more recently, "Ontario, there's no taste like home."

The increasing availability and promotion of local food growers and products in Canada is also evidenced by the enormous amount of information now available to consumers. Media promotions range from the publication and public distribution of local "food maps," such as Simcoe County Farm Fresh's *Buy Fresh Buy Local: Your Year-Round Guide to Buying Local Food* (2010) — maps which locate farmers, producers, restaurants, farmers' markets, and local food retailers — to numerous websites sponsored by non-profit as well as government agencies. Despite the overwhelming complexities of global economics, then, such changes in our own communities suggest the capacity for individual consumers to effect potentially major changes in the production and consumption of food at both local and global levels. Further, these avenues for "consumer power" also provide alternative social spaces in which changing our relationship to food becomes a process of changing cultural patterns and beliefs.

While the average consumer may not feel very powerful and largely a recipient of what the large corporations dish out, evidence that individual consumers can change some of the largest companies in the world continues to be made visible even in major supermarkets. Citing the example of Wal-Mart's unprecedented move to stock milk with no synthetic hormones in response to consumer demand, Robert Kenner convincingly insisted in his documentary, *Food inc.*, that consumers "have the ability to change the world with every bite" (Kenner & Pearlstein, 2008).

Defining "Local"

Defining "local," however, is problematic. Do eggs produced by local chickens fed on imported grains, for example, still qualify as local food? Further, as several recent studies have suggested, the idea of "local" is socially constructed, complicated by issues related to specific geographical

THE LOCAL FOOD MOVEMENT IN CANADA   6

locations, socioeconomic factors, retail marketing strategies, and consumer awareness and practices (Blake, Mellor, & Crane, 2010, p. 409). The complicated rhetorical status of "local" or "the discursive association of 'local' with trust, shared norms and values" (Blake, Mellor, & Crane, 2010, p. 410), has recently come under critical examination. Lori Stahlbrand, head of Toronto's Local Food Plus organization, argued that "local alone does not recognize issues of sustainability, animal welfare, labour practices, biodiversity and energy use" (Cuthbert, 2008, p. 58).

In his engagement with the recent critique of the local food movement, Jesse McEntee (2010) distinguished between "contemporary" and "traditional" localism, practices divided by socioeconomic considerations. The "contemporary local," McEntee argued, "is represented by current local food initiatives and fits within the umbrella of alternative food networks sometimes associated with middle and upper class consumers" (p. 786) and involves activities with ideological labels attached. Paralleling and sometimes intersecting contemporary localism, "traditional localism" is not guided by ideological considerations but simply "by a motivation to obtain fresh and affordable food and/or continue traditional modes of food production" (McEntee, 2010, p. 786).

The concept of "local" in the context of the products sold at Canadian farmers' markets has also come under scrutiny. In his report on the reopening of the Hamilton Farmers' Market, "Thinking Local, Acting Loco?" (2011), Andrew Potter claimed that the rejection of numerous applications of previous long-term vendors such as Vietnamese and Middle Eastern food sellers was the result of the Market's "rebranding [and] pitching itself at the yuppie constituency" (p. 65), giving priority to vendors whose goods were organically produced within a 100-mile radius. Potter argued that such a revamping dangerously dismisses the fact that the Hamilton Farmers' Market has historically been responsive as a community to the influx of immigrant vendors, thus informing what Hamiltonians understand as "local" (p. 66)....

[Text continues in full report]

THE LOCAL FOOD MOVEMENT IN CANADA   7

❶ Food miles. As Smith and MacKinnon (2007) reported, "according to the Leopold Center for Sustainable Agriculture at Iowa State University, the food we eat now typically travels between 1,500 and 3,000 miles from farm to plate" (p. 3). Buying local food, then, is promoted not only as a way of choosing fresher and healthier foods, and supporting local farmers and local economies, but also as a way of reducing food miles, shortening the supply chains, and helping to preserve the environment. Similar to the call for a closer examination of what is meant by "local," however, the demand for further detailed mapping of the distance "from farm to fork" and for an analysis of the specific environmental costs of producing and distributing local as compared to imported foods has led to a more critical examination of food miles in discussions of local food activism.

The issues are more complicated than how far food travels. Following their investigation of food miles, researchers at Lincoln University in New Zealand "concluded that dairy raised in New Zealand and shipped to Britain actually had a smaller carbon footprint than the U.K.'s own dairy" (Cuthbert, 2008, p. 58). In their study of what "local" means in the context of farmers' markets in British Columbia, Ling and Newman (2011) introduced food webs that show a large variation in the distances travelled from farm to market, since the 123 farmers' markets in the province were primarily located on the lower B.C. mainland and the south-east coast of Vancouver Island (Ling & Newman, 2011, Figure 1). Their study suggested that food miles were not necessarily significantly reduced through the advocacy of farmers' markets. Further, Morrison, Nelson, and Ostry (2010) argued that while the promotion of local food security has increased in the last decade, "methods to empirically access the types and quantities of crops and animals produced locally (i.e., local food production capacity) were underdeveloped, hindering the ability of policy makers to effect innovative local food security policy" (p. 491).

For **third-level headings**, indent, bold, capitalize the first letter only, and end with a period; start text immediately following heading **❶**

Do not start a new page for **subsections** (e.g., "Conclusion")

J

THE LOCAL FOOD MOVEMENT IN CANADA 8

Farmers' Markets

The *Orillia Farmers' Market* website, as in numerous local food websites, lists key reasons to shop at farmers' markets, including the value of knowing your food source, supporting family farmers, protecting the environment, and connecting with your community. Yet in their study and survey of 15 farmers' markets in Ontario, Smithers, Lamarche, and Joseph (2008) found a significant discrepancy between the expectations, assumptions, and demands of sellers, shoppers, and managers. Unexamined assumptions of the quality, authenticity, and legitimacy of both vendors and their products revealed "local" as a variable term, "widely valued but also highly interpretive in its meaning" (Smithers, Lamarche, & Joseph, 2008, p. 337).... [Text continues in full report]

J **Conclusion**

The concept of food sovereignty evolved from the increasing global critique of international agricultural policies introduced in the 1980s and early 1990s.

The term "food sovereignty" was coined to recognize the political and economic power dimension inherent in the food and agriculture debate and to take a pro-active stance by naming it. Food sovereignty, broadly defined as the right of nations and peoples to control their own food systems, including their own markets, production modes, food cultures and environments, has emerged as a critical alternative to the dominant neoliberal model for agriculture and trade. (Wittman, Desmarais, & Wiebe, 2010, p. 2)

The local food movement, then, addresses the issue of food security as an issue of social justice and equity. Hamm and Bellows defined community food security as "a situation in which all community residents obtain a safe, culturally acceptable, nutritionally adequate diet through a sustainable food system that maximizes community self-reliance and social justice" (as cited in McEntee, 2010, p. 786). The philosophy of "relocalization" has motivated government policy changes as well as numbers of initiatives worldwide that often provide small-scale and regional solutions to what are, nevertheless, global problems (Miller, 2008, p. 145).

THE LOCAL FOOD MOVEMENT IN CANADA   9

In Canada, for example, farmers' markets, community gardens, community-supported agriculture, and good food boxes organized by non-profit groups such as Vancouver's Farm Folk/City Folk and Toronto's Farm Share contribute to the global effort of food activists to redress the inequities of a corporatized food system and to build community health. Several non-profit organizations in Canadian urban centres promote food security for their communities not only by providing access to fresh produce and common gardens but also through educational programs aimed to empower and inform their local residents. As Canada's largest community food security organization, Toronto's FoodShare, for example, claims to "reach over 145,000 children and adults a month through subsidized fresh produce distribution, student nutrition programs, community gardening and cooking, classroom curriculum support, homemade baby food workshops and youth internships" ("About FoodShare," 2012).... [Text continues in full report]

Although further studies are needed to assess the viability of local food production and distribution, the reduction of food miles, and the role and effectiveness of farmers' markets in the local food movement, evidence of an active resistance to the current industrialized food system exists in a local food movement in Canada. This movement involves both activists and community members seeking informed and alternative ways to promote access to healthy foods, environmental sustainability, and food security for their communities. In this movement, as Robert Kenner (2008) argued, consumer power cannot be underestimated. In his informative and eye-opening documentary, *Food, inc.*, Kenner ended with a series of imperatives for the viewer and common consumer: "When you go to the supermarket choose foods that are in season. Buy foods that are organic. Know what's in your food. Read labels.... Buy foods that are grown locally. Shop at farmers' markets. Plant a garden (even a small one). You can change the world with every bite" (Kenner & Pearlstein, 2008).

Sample References Page

Begin a new page for the list of references.

A Include the **running head** and **page number**

B **Centre** the word **"References"** at the top of the page

C Set the **first line** of each entry **flush left** and **indent subsequent lines**

D **Double space** all lines

E List each entry **alphabetically** (according to the **first letter** of each entry)

A THE LOCAL FOOD MOVEMENT IN CANADA   10

B References

C About FoodShare: Our approach and our impacts. (2012). *FoodShare*. Retrieved from http://www.foodshare.net/

Blake, M. K., Mellor, J., & Crane, L. (2010, March). Buying local food: Shopping practices, place, and consumption networks in defining **D** food as "local." *Annals of the Association of American Geographers, 100*(2), 409–426.

Cuthbert, P. (2008, March 17). Local schmocal. *Maclean's, 121*(10), 57–58.

E Eaton, E. (2008). From feeding the locals to selling the locale: Adapting local sustainable food projects in Niagara to neocommunitarianism and neoliberalism. *Geoforum, 39*, 994–1006. http://dx.doi.org /10.1016/j.geoforum.2007.10.017

Kenner, R. (Producer/Director), & Pearlstein, E. (Producer). (2008). *Food, inc.* [DVD]. United States: Alliance Films.

Lawrence, G., Lyons, K., & Wallington, T. (Eds.). (2010). *Food security, nutrition and sustainability*. London, United Kingdom: Earthscan.

Lawrence, G., Lyons, K., & Wallington, T. (2010). Introduction: Food security, nutrition and sustainability in a globalized world. In *Food security, nutrition and sustainability*. London, United Kingdom: Earthscan.

Ling, C., & Newman, L. L. (2011). Untangling the food web: Farm-to-market distances in British Columbia, Canada. *Local Environment: The International Journal of Justice and Sustainability, 16*, 807–822.

McEntee, J. (2010, October/November). Contemporary and traditional localism: A conceptualization of rural local food. *Local Environment, 15*, 785–803. doi:10.1080/13549839.2010.509390

THE LOCAL FOOD MOVEMENT IN CANADA   11

Miller, S. (2008). *Edible action: Food activism & alternative economics.*
    Halifax, Canada: Fernwood.

Morrison, K. T., Nelson, T. A., & Ostry, A. S. (2011). Methods for
    mapping local food production capacity from agricultural statistics.
    Agricultural Systems, 104, 491–499. http://dx.doi.org/10.1016/j
    .agsy.2011.03.006

Potter, A. (2011, January 17). Thinking local, acting loco? *Maclean's,*
    124(1), 65–66.

Simcoe County Farm Fresh Marketing Association. (2010). *Buy fresh*
    buy local: Your year-round guide to buying local food [Map]. Barrie,
    Canada: Author.

Smith, A., & MacKinnon, J. B. (2007). *The 100-mile diet: A year of local*
    eating. Toronto, Canada: Random House.

Smithers, J., Lamarche, J., & Joseph, A. E. (2008). Unpacking the
    terms of engagement with local food at the farmers' market: Insights
    from Ontario. *Journal of Rural Studies, 24,* 337–350. http://dx.doi
    .org/10.1016/j.jrurstud.2007.12.009

Statistics Canada. (2012). *Highlights and analyses of the 2011 census*
    of agriculture. Retrieved from http://www.statcan.gc/pub/95-640
    -x/2012002/05-eng.htm

Werkerle, G. R. (2004). Food justice movements: Policy, planning, and
    networks. *Journal of Planning and Education Research, 23*(4),
    378–386. doi:10.1177/0739456X04264886

What we do. (2012). *FoodShare.* Retrieved from http://www.foodshare
    .net/

Wittman, H., Desmarais, A. A., & Wiebe, N. (Eds.). (2010). *Food*
    sovereignty: Reconnecting food, nature and community. Halifax,
    Canada: Fernwood.

List each entry **alphabetically** (according to the **first letter** of each entry)

3 Citing Sources

"… maples turned scarlet across the pond, beneath where the white stems of three aspens diverged, at the point of a promontory, next to the water. Ah, many a tale their color told! And gradually from week to week the character of each tree came out, and it admired itself reflected in the smooth mirror of the lake. Each morning the manager of this gallery substituted some new picture, distinguished by more brilliant or harmonious coloring, for the old upon the walls."

Henry David Thoreau, 1854

Thoreau, H. D. (2004). *Walden* (J. S. Cramer, Ed.). New Haven, CT: Yale University Press. (Original work published 1854)

Photo © Heather Holm

Citing Sources

You must acknowledge any ideas or facts used to write your paper by using in-text citations. In-text citations enclose in parentheses the author and date of any sources consulted in your research and include page numbers for direct quotations.

IN-TEXT CITATIONS

An In-Text Citation:
1 Identifies your **research source** for a quotation or paraphrased information.
2 **Leads readers** to the References list at the end of your paper for **further information** on the research source.

TWO WAYS TO CITE

Direct Quotation:

Uses **exact words** from your source and always includes the source's page number.

Paraphrase:

Uses your **own words to summarize** or **rephrase** the source's idea(s). In most instances, page numbers are recommended to lead an interested reader directly to the paraphrased passage.

A CITATION
1 Follows an **idea or fact** taken from a research source.
2 Includes (within parentheses) the **author's surname**, **publication date**, and **page number(s)**.
3 Is normally **placed at the end of the sentence**. The punctuation for the sentence follows the citation.

Building a Citation

A citation acknowledges and documents the research source you used to emphasize, reinforce, or prove any point you made in your research paper.

If a source is in your References list, there must be an in-text citation for that source in your paper and vice versa. Students whose research papers do not cite sources could be liable for plagiarism and face severe academic penalties! See pp. 7–11.

BASIC AUTHOR-DATE
A citation in APA style follows the author-date method.

(Author, Date) (Kandel, 2012)

AUTHOR, NO DATE
If there is no date available for the citation, the abbreviation n.d. is used.

(Author, n.d.) (Didier, n.d.)

NO AUTHOR
If there is no author identified for the citation, use the first few words of the title followed by the year of publication.

(Title, Date) ("Patent Trials," 2012)

DIRECT QUOTATION/PARAPHRASE
The citation following a direct quotation must include the page numbers; in most instances, page numbers are recommended to lead an interested reader directly to the paraphrased passage.

(Author, Date, p. #) (Kandel, 2012, p. 47)

ELECTRONIC SOURCES
Often electronic sources, such as websites and e-books, do not provide page numbers. In this case, use the paragraph number, preceded by "para." If neither paragraph nor page numbers are included, cite the heading (if lengthy, a shortened version in quotation marks) to direct the reader to the location of your source material.

(Author, Date, para. #) (Statistics Canada, 2012, para. 21)

Using Direct Quotations

Work direct quotations into the grammatical structure and logic of your own sentences. Clearly **indicate the relevance** of the quoted material to your discussion. Never insert a quotation without an introduction.

Provide the **author's name, the publication year, and the page number** in an in-text citation directly following the quotation.

SHORT QUOTATIONS

Incorporate a short, direct quotation (fewer than 40 words) **directly into the text** of your paper and enclose it in **double quotation marks**. If you introduce the author in the text of your paper directly before the quotation, you do not need to include the author's name in your parenthetical citation (as in the second example).

Example 1

Confederation is still a sore issue with many Newfoundlanders. The campaign to join Canada was characterized as "the route a good Newfoundlander would take to benefit his people" (Thompson, 1980, p. 23).

Example 2

Confederation is still a sore issue with many Newfoundlanders. According to R. C. Thompson (1980), the campaign to join Canada was characterized as "the route a good Newfoundlander would take to benefit his people" (p. 23).

Note that the period *follows* the citation at the end of a short quotation.

LONG QUOTATIONS

Set off longer quotations (40 words or more) from the rest of your written text by **block indenting** the quotation one tab from the left margin. Double-space the entire quotation and do not enclose it in quotation marks.

Example

The concept of food sovereignty evolved from the increasing global critique of international agricultural policies introduced in the 1980s and early 1990s.

> The term "food sovereignty" was coined to recognize the political and economic power dimension inherent in the food and agriculture debate and to take a pro-active stance by naming it. Food sovereignty, broadly defined as the right of nations and peoples to control their own food systems, including their own markets, production modes, food cultures and environments, has emerged as a critical alternative to the dominant neoliberal model for agriculture and trade. (Wittman, Desmarais, & Wiebe, 2010, p. 2)

Note that the period is placed *before* the in-text citation in a long quotation. Use double quotation marks to enclose text cited in quotation marks in the original text, as in the example above.

Paraphrasing

Paraphrasing an idea means putting the author's ideas into your own words.

WHEN PARAPHRASING, YOU MUST:

Include the author's name and the publication date in parentheses following the paraphrased material.

In most instances, page numbers are recommended to lead an interested reader directly to the paraphrased passage. Consult your instructor or professor.

PARAPHRASE

If you introduce the author in the text of your paper, you do not need to include the author's name in your reference (as in Example 2).

Example 1

The philosophy of "relocalization" has motivated government policy changes as well as numbers of local food initiatives worldwide that often provide small-scale and regional solutions to what are, nevertheless, global problems (Miller, 2008, p. 145).

Example 2

Miller (2008) pointed out that despite the small-scale, personal, and regional nature of many local food initiatives, the impact on food production and distribution, policy changes, consumer practice, and community health has been substantial (p. 145).

Example of Paraphrasing Within a Report or Research Paper

Increasing consumer awareness of the need for healthy, cost-effective, and environmentally sustainable food production has, in part, as Morrison, Nelson, and Ostry (2011) argued, grown out of the "emergence of periodic food safety crises [that] have alarmed the public" such as "mad cow" disease, the contamination of milk in China, and an outbreak of Listeriosis at a Maple Leaf Foods' Canadian processing plant (p. 491). Moreover, it is estimated that in the United States one in three children born after 2000 will contract early onset diabetes (Kenner & Perlstein, 2008).

In-Text References to Books and Articles

The rules for CAPITALIZING and *italicizing* in the text or body of your report or essay are **different** from those you should follow for your citations (parenthetical information) and for your References list entries.

IN-TEXT REFERENCES TO BOOKS, FILMS, BROCHURES, AND PERIODICALS (ENTIRE WORKS)

To refer to a book, film, brochure, or periodical (an entire magazine or newspaper), **CAPITALIZE** the **first letter** of each word in the **title** and *italicize* the title. Do not capitalize articles ("a" and "an"), prepositions ("in," "at," etc.), or conjunctions ("but," "and," "or") unless they are the first word of a title, the word following a colon, or a word of four letters or more.

> D. A. Wilson (2011), in the second volume of his biography, *Thomas D'Arcy McGee: The Extreme Moderate, 1857–1868*, recounted McGee's passionate dedication to uniting Canada.

IN-TEXT REFERENCES TO ARTICLES AND CHAPTERS

To refer to an article or chapter from a book or periodical, **CAPITALIZE** the **first letter** of each word in the **title** and place the title in **quotation marks**.

> Corstjens and Lal (2012) cautioned in their article "Retail Doesn't Cross Borders: Here's Why and What to Do About It" that international expansion does not necessarily mean greater profits.

4 Using In-Text Citations

"That whimsical fellow called Evolution, having enlarged the dinosaur until he tripped over his own toes, tried shrinking the chickadee until he was just too big to be snapped up by flycatchers as an insect, and just too little to be pursued by hawks and owls as meat."

Aldo Leopold, 1949

Leopold, A. (2001). *A Sand County almanac*. New York, NY: Oxford University Press.
   (Original work published 1949)

Photo © Heather Holm

Using In-Text Citations

APA requires the author-date method of citation. Periods, commas, and semicolons are placed **outside** the citation (with the exception of a quotation of 40 or more words). The following lists some guidelines and examples.

Articles in Books or Periodicals

Magazines, journals, and newspapers are considered "periodicals." The following examples show how to cite references to ideas and facts from books and/or periodicals.

1 SINGLE AUTHOR

Cite the **author's surname**, the **date of publication**, and **page number**.

Along with Breuer, Freud was credited with developing psychoanalysis "as a dynamic, introspective psychology, a precursor of modern cognitive psychology" (Kandel, 2012, p. 47).

2 SINGLE AUTHOR (SIGNAL PHRASE)

If you indicate the author's name in the body of your sentence, cite only the **date of publication**.

Kandel in his recently published book (2012) brought together theories of art, science, and mind.

3 MULTIPLE WORKS BY ONE AUTHOR

List multiple works by one author within a single set of parentheses in **chronological order**.

Northrop Frye's numerous publications on education reflect his lifelong commitment to the value of teaching literature (Frye, 1963, 1967, 1988, 1990).

4 MULTIPLE WORKS BY ONE AUTHOR WITH THE SAME DATE

Use **suffixes** (a, b, c, and so on) to identify **multiple works by one author** published in the same year. In the References list, order these works **alphabetically by title, and include the particular suffix assigned to the year**.

That year he published several studies on education as well as literary criticism (Frye, 1963a, 1963b, 1963c).

5 NO AUTHOR

Cite a few **key words from the title** followed by the **year of publication**. Enclose an article or chapter title in double quotation marks and use italics for titles of books, films, periodicals, brochures, or reports.

A copyright trial with monumental implications for the technology industry is unfolding in a U.S. court. Oracle Corp. has charged that Google Inc. "stole its intellectual property to make Android software" ("Patent Trials," 2012, p. B4).

An editorial argues that forms of social media, such as Facebook and MySpace, are current examples of creative minds taking advantage of opportunity, timing and the right conditions, all key factors required for innovation and new inventions ("Steam Engine Time," 2012, p. 3).

6 TWO AUTHORS

Cite both **authors' surnames** joined by "**&**".

Despite the fact that large grocery retailers want to expand internationally, evidence proves there has been little success to date in their efforts. A *Harvard Business Review* article noted that "When we [the authors] focused on one industry — grocery retailing — we found that, with a few exceptions, globalization's benefits had not accrued to retailers" (Corstjens & Lal, 2012, p. 104).

Use square brackets inside the quotation marks to enclose information not in the original. In this instance, square brackets enclose explanatory information necessary to understand the full meaning of the quotation.

7 THREE TO FIVE AUTHORS

Cite all the **authors' surnames in the first citation**. For **subsequent citations**, include only the **surname of the first author** followed by "**et al**." and the year: (Guffey et al., 2011).

Clarity and conciseness are two major principles of effective business writing (Guffey, Rhodes, & Rogin, 2011).

8 SIX OR MORE AUTHORS

For first and subsequent citations, cite only the **surname of the first author** followed by "**et al**." and the year.

As reported in an issue of *Canadian Medical Association Journal*, a recent research study found the diagnosis of ADHD in British Columbia for children 6 to 12 years "consistent with a relative-age effect" (Morrow et al., 2012, p. 759). The study concluded that "children born during the month preceding the province's cut-off date for entry to school are typically the youngest and least mature within their grade, and are at a higher risk for treatment and diagnosis of ADHD" (Morrow et al., 2012, p. 759).

9 TWO OR MORE WORKS BY DIFFERENT AUTHORS

To cite several studies by different authors, cite the **authors' names in alphabetical order** inside **one set of parentheses**. Separate the citations by **semicolons**.

Several recent studies (Miller, 2008; Smithers, Lamarche, & Joseph, 2008; Wittman, Desmarais, & Wiebe, 2010) have suggested that the growing public support in Canada of local food production is part of a broader political and social movement for changes in international policies to address a global agri-food crisis.

10 GROUP OR CORPORATE AUTHOR

Groups as authors include government agencies, corporations, businesses, and associations. Cite the **full name of the group** in the first and following citations. However, if the group name is lengthy and well known, add the abbreviation in square brackets following the first citation and use only the **abbreviation** for subsequent citations.

In a recent policy paper (2012), the union for auto workers in Canada argued for a "change in philosophy and direction" on the part of provincial governments and the federal government in Canada in order for the industry to "rebuild a viable new auto industry that can provide good jobs for another generation of Canadians" (Canadian Auto Workers [CAW], p. 49).

This policy paper (2012) argued that Canada's auto industry must receive support from government rather than rely only on market forces (CAW, p. 49).

Note the use of the well-known abbreviation CAW for the corporate author, Canadian Auto Workers, in the second example.

11 NO DATE

Use "**n.d.**" if no date of publication is available.

A very helpful brochure provides a range of information about health services in Ontario communities (Ontario Ministry of Health, n.d.).

12 SPECIFIC PARTS OF A SECONDARY SOURCE

To cite a part of a work, indicate the **Chapter**, **Figure**, or **Table**.

The 123 farmers' markets in the province are primarily located on the lower B.C. mainland and the south-east coast of Vancouver Island (Ling & Newman, 2011, Figure 1).

Lawrence, Lyons, and Wallington (2010) provided a comprehensive overview of the diverse issues involved in any theoretical or practical approach to addressing food security and sustainability (Chapter 1).

13 WORK DISCUSSED IN A SECONDARY SOURCE

Cite the source from which you are quoting rather than the original source referenced. In the body of your paper, clearly state the **author** and **work** that your source text references. For example, to include a quotation by Hamm and Bellows found in an article by McEntee, cite McEntee, **not** Hamm and Bellows as your source.

Popular concepts of food security imply issues of social justice and equity, as in Hamm and Bellows' definition of community food security as "a situation in which all community residents obtain a safe, culturally acceptable, nutritionally adequate diet through a sustainable food system that maximizes community self-reliance and social justice" (as cited in McEntee, 2010, p. 786).

Note the use of "as cited in" in the example above of a direct quotation taken from another source. Make use of "as cited in" sparingly, for example, with an out-of-print work or a work difficult to find for use as a primary reference.

14 CITATION WITHIN A QUOTATION

When quoting in your paper, **include citations made within the original material**. Include these citations in your final References list only if you have used them as original sources elsewhere in your paper.

Consumer awareness of the need for healthy, cost-effective, and environmentally sustainable food production has, in part, grown out of the "emergence of periodic food safety crises [that] have alarmed the public; for example, Avian influenza, Bovine spongiform encephalopathy ('mad cow' disease), the recent outbreak of melamine contamination of milk in China, and an outbreak of Listeriosis at a Maple Leaf Foods' Canadian processing plant (Joffe & Lee, 2004; Wilson & Keelan, 2008)" (Morrison, Nelson, & Ostry, 2011, p. 491).

15 QUOTATION WITHIN A QUOTATION

If there is a **quotation within a source** you are quoting, use **single quotation marks** to set off the in-source quoted material. Enclose your complete quoted text in double quotation marks.

In 2008, *The Globe and Mail* reported a recall of the drug heparin. A spokesperson for the company involved announced that "patients who have the product 'should discontinue use immediately,' but added that the product is used almost exclusively in hospitals" (Picard, p. A9).

16 CLASSIC WORKS

When citing old works, cite both the **original publication date** and the **date of your version**. For example, to cite the novel *Frankenstein*, by Mary Shelley, originally published in 1818 and republished in 2000, cite (Shelley, 1818/2000).

The original opening of *Frankenstein* sets the stage for the telling of a classic ghost story: "It was on a dreary night of November that I beheld the accomplishment of my toils" (Shelley, 1818/2000, p. 60).

For very old works for which the date of publication is unavailable, cite the year of the translation or version you used, preceded by "trans." or followed by "version," for example (Plato, trans. 1955).

17 PARTS OF CLASSIC WORKS

Refer to parts of major classical works (Greek and Roman works, the Bible, Shakespeare, and so on) **in the text of your paper by part** (e.g., books, chapters, verses, lines, cantos). Identify the **version** in the **first citation** only.

Classic works such as ancient Greek works and the Bible are not listed in your References list.

In the Bible, the passage often read at weddings from 1 Corinthians 13:1–13 speaks of the role of faith, hope, and love (New Revised Standard Version).

Electronic Sources

Use the same format to cite electronic sources as you would to cite a print source. See **Section 3: Citing Sources**.

If an electronic document does not indicate the name of the author(s), place in the author position either a **shortened version of the title** or the **name of the organization** that published the document. Readers will know to look in the **References** list under the term chosen in place of the author.

18 SINGLE AUTHOR

Cite the **author's surname** and the date of publication (or the **date of update/date of retrieval**).

More research is required to understand the connections between the motivation to perform activities and passion (Vallerand, 2012).

19 NO AUTHOR

If no individual author of a website document is indicated, use either a **shortened version of the title** or the **name of the organization, group, or website publisher**.

An educated workforce provides many benefits to Canadian society ("Investing Crucial," 2012).

Organic farm operations in Canada increased from 0.9% in 2001 to 1.8% in 2011 according to the recent Census of Agriculture (Statistics Canada, 2011, para. 21).

20 MULTIPLE AUTHORS

Follow the **same directions** as those for citing multiple authors in **print format**.

Employers' health and wellness programs should have focus and measured outcomes in order to produce return on investment (Cyboran & Goldsmith, 2012).

21 NO DATE

Use "**n.d.**" if no date of publication is available.

Although there are many ways to define sustainable agriculture, efforts are being made to create a national standard (Didier, n.d.).

22 NO PAGE NUMBER

For websites and e-books not providing page numbers, use a **paragraph number** (e.g., "para. 21"). If no paragraph number is available or appropriate, use a **heading**, in quotation marks and shortened if lengthy (e.g., "About FoodShare"), to direct the reader to the source.

In addition, organic farm operations in Canada increased from 0.9% in 2001 to 1.8% in 2011 according to the recent Census of Agriculture (Statistics Canada, 2012, para. 21).

As Canada's largest community food security organization, Toronto's FoodShare programs "reach over 145,000 children and adults per month in Toronto" ("About FoodShare," 2012) through subsidized fresh produce distribution, student nutrition programs, community gardening and cooking, classroom curriculum support, homemade baby food workshops, and youth internships.

Other Publications

23 COMIC STRIP/PHOTOGRAPH/ILLUSTRATION

Cite the source of the comic strip, photograph, or illustration as you would a print source.

The "Backbench: MP's – Off the Record" comic strip takes a satirical view of federal politics in Canada by poking fun at pension review (Harrop, 2012, p. R6).

The 123 farmers' markets in the province are primarily located on the lower B.C. mainland and the south-east coast of Vancouver Island (Ling & Newman, 2011, Figure 1).

24 FILM/DVD/TELEVISION BROADCAST

Place the producer, director, and/or scriptwriter in the **author** position. Use the **release date** for the date.

The film *Monsieur Lazhar* recounts the story of an Algerian refugee who, while battling his own traumatic memories, takes a job as a public school teacher in Montreal (Dery, McCraw, & Falaradeau, 2011).

25 DICTIONARY/ENCYCLOPEDIA DEFINITION

If the entry is unsigned (no author), use the **first few words of the title of the entry** from the dictionary or encyclopedia in place of the author's name.

Hypercalcemic nephropathy is defined as "a progressive disorder of kidney function caused by an excessive level of calcium in the blood" ("Hypercalcemic Nephropathy," 2009, p. 906).

26 PERSONAL COMMUNICATIONS

Personal communications include **interviews, lectures, telephone conversations, letters, memos,** and **some electronic communications** such as e-mail and messages from non-archived discussion groups.

Personal communications are **cited only in-text**, not in the References list, **unless** the item is a **recoverable electronic communication**.

In the citation, include the **initials and the surname** of the communicator, as well as a full date.

As a registered massage therapist explained, "Therapeutic massage is an important part of our health care and is playing an ever-increasing role in the improvement of people's health" (K. Mackay, personal communication, June 9, 2012).

5 Preparing Your References List

"... I happened to look down to the mossy shelf below and there in the shade made the discovery of the day, a single pink lady-slipper in full bloom. While I looked at it, I forgot the heat and humidity and thought of the great woods to the south where its closest kin, the showy lady-slipper is found, and of all the great solitudes of the earth where members of the orchis family bloom. Alike in their needs, no matter where they grow, in the depths of tropical jungles or in the woods of the north, shadows and solitudes are part of their lives. They are flowers of primeval and the unchanged places of the earth."

Sigurd F. Olson, 1958

Olson, S. F. (1958). *Listening point.* New York, NY: Alfred A. Knopf.

Photo © Heather Holm

Preparing Your References List

In the References page, list all of the sources cited within the text of your paper.

Do not include materials consulted in your research that were not directly cited in your paper.

The examples below reflect information available from the *Publication Manual of the American Psychological Association, Sixth Edition, APA Style Guide to Electronic References, Sixth Edition,* and http://blog.apastyle.org.

INCLUDING A DIGITAL OBJECT IDENTIFIER (DOI) IN REFERENCES LIST ENTRIES

A **Digital Object Identifier (DOI)** is an alphanumeric code for both print and online articles and materials, e.g., doi:10.1016j.bbi2007.12.002 and http://dx.doi.org/10.1097/01.NAJ.0000413457.53110.3a. It acts as a fixed identifier/link to scholarly content. **No further retrieval information is required if a DOI is available.** Include it in the reference entry **exactly as it appears** in the document.

DOIs are usually found on the first page of a journal article or a document such as a PDF file. Some databases may hide the DOI behind a button marked "Article" or "PubMed." CrossRef.org provides a link resolver to find material through a DOI, as well as to check if an item has been assigned a DOI.

Copy and paste the DOI into the References list to ensure its integrity.

Print or Online/Database Article (With DOI)

Include the DOI, if available, and in the format provided for both print and online sources.

> Iezzoni, L. I., & Ogg, M. (2012). Patient's perspective: Hard lessons from a long hospital stay. *American Journal of Nursing, 112*(4), 39–42. http://dx.doi.org/10.1097/01.NAJ.0000413457.53110.3a
>
> Vallerand, R. J. (2012). From motivation to passion: In search of the motivational processes involved in a meaningful life. *Canadian Psychology, 53*(1), 42–52. doi:10.1037/a0026377

Print Article (No DOI)

MacLellan, L. (2012, February). In the company of strangers. *Report on Business, 28*(7), 14–16.

Online/Database Article (No DOI)

If an article with no DOI is found in a database, a web search is required to find either the direct link (full URL) or the journal's, magazine's, newspaper's, or publisher's home page URL. Use either the direct link or home page URL, whichever is more dependable, in your retrieval statement.

Chapman, S. (2012, September). Manufacturing taste. *The Walrus, 9*(7). Retrieved from http://walrusmagazine.com/articles /2012.09-food-manufacturing-taste/7/

Chapman, S. (2012, September). Manufacturing taste. *The Walrus, 9*(7). Retrieved from http://walrusmagazine.com

Article Available ONLY in a Database (No DOI)

In the retrieval statement include the most reliable method of retrieval from the following options: the journal's home page URL, the database home page URL, or the database name and accession number (no URL).

Statham, T. R. (2011). *Dogma and history in Victorian Scotland* (Doctoral dissertation). Available from ProQuest Dissertations and Theses. (AAT NR 74796)

Thompson, K. J., Thach, E. C., & Morelli, M. (2010). Implementing ethical leadership: Current challenges and solutions. *Insights to a Changing World Journal*, (4), 107–130. Retrieved from http://www.ebscohost.com/academic/academic-search-complete

Thompson, K. J., Thach, E. C., & Morelli, M. (2010). Implementing ethical leadership: Current challenges and solutions. *Insights to a Changing World Journal*, (4), 107–130. Retrieved from http://www.franklinpublishing.net/insightstoachangingworld.html

Building a Reference Entry

Think of each part of a reference entry as a unit. Each unit is separated by a period or a comma.

BOOK				
Author.	(Date).	*Title of book.*	Location:	Publisher.

Kandel, E. R. (2012). *The age of insight: The quest to understand the unconscious in art, mind, and brain, from Vienna 1900 to the present.* New York, NY: Random House.

PERIODICAL (PRINT OR ONLINE)						
Author.	(Date).	Title of article.	*Title of Periodical,*	Volume(Issue),	Page(s).	DOI (if available)

Iezzoni, L. I., & Ogg, M. (2012). Patient's perspective: Hard lessons from a long hospital stay. *American Journal of Nursing, 112*(4), 39–42. http://dx.doi.org/10.1097/01 .NAJ.0000413457.53110.3a

PERIODICAL (NO AUTHOR)					
Title of article.	(Date).	*Title of Periodical,*	Volume(Issue),	Page(s).	DOI (if available)

Borderviews: Light plain/plane of light. (2012, March/April/May). *Border Crossings, 31*(1), 18.

ONLINE/DATABASE ARTICLE (NO DOI)						
Author.	(Date).	Title of article.	*Title of Periodical,*	Volume(Issue),	Page(s).	Retrieval Statement

Jennings, H., Nedeljkovic, M., & Moulding, R. (2011). The influence of confidence in memory on checking behaviours. *E-Journal of Applied Psychology, 7*(2), 9–16. Retrieved from http://ojs.lib .swin.edu.au/index.php/ejap/article/view/192/278

ARTICLE AVAILABLE ONLY IN A DATABASE (NO DOI)						
Author.	(Date).	Title of article.	*Title of Periodical,*	Volume(Issue),	Page(s).	Retrieval Statement

Thompson, K. J., Thach, E. C., & Morelli, M. (2010). Implementing ethical leadership: Current challenges and solutions. *Insights to a Changing World Journal,* (4), 107–130. Retrieved from http://www.franklinpublishing.net/insightstoachangingworld.html

Setting up a References Page

A List entries alphabetically, set the first line of each entry flush left, and indent subsequent lines

B Capitalize the first letter of a word that follows a colon

C When the author and the publisher are the same, use "Author" as the publisher

D Use (n.d.) if there is no date of publication

E In the retrieval statement, use either the direct link URL or the journal's/website's home page URL when there is no DOI

F Provide the screen name as posted in square brackets following the user's real name, if known

G Italicize the titles of print, audiovisual, and online works (books, journals, newspapers, magazines, reports, web documents, brochures, films, DVDs, and television and radio productions)

H Include the issue number in parentheses immediately following the volume number of a journal that begins each issue with page 1

I Do not use "p." or "pp." for articles in magazines or scholarly journals

---

References

A Aucoin, P., Jarvis, M. D., & Turnbull, L. (2011). *Democratizing the Constitution: Reforming responsible government.* Toronto, Canada: Edmond Montgomery.

Canadian Auto Workers. (2012). *Re-thinking Canada's auto industry:* **B** *A policy vision to escape the race to the bottom.* Toronto, **C** Canada: Author.

Didier, S. **D** (n.d.). What does sustainable food mean? *National Geographic.* **E** Retrieved from http://greenliving .nationalgeographic.com/sustainable-food-mean-2944.html

F Harper, S. [Stephen]. (2012, March 14). Launched the Vimy Foundation Pin Campaign to raise awareness of the Battle of Vimy Ridge. Lest we forget: http://ow.ly/9F9KK [Tweet]. Retrieved from https://twitter.com/#!/pmharper

Iezzoni, L. I., & Ogg, M. (2012). Patient's perspective: Hard lessons from a long hospital stay. *American Journal of Nursing,* **G** *112*(4), **H** **I** 39–42. http://dx.doi.org/10.1097/01.NAJ.0000413457 .53110.3a

For entries that begin with "A," "An," or "The," alphabetize by the first letter of the second word

J

Capitalize the first letter only of a non-periodical (books, brochures, web documents, audio-visual productions)

K

Enclose non-routine information in square brackets immediately after the title and before the period

L

Use "&" to join the surnames of the last two authors

M

Capitalize the first letter only of the title of an article

N

Italicize volume numbers and do not use "Vol." before the number

O

J The Law Society of Upper Canada. (n.d.). **K** *Looking for a lawyer?* **L** [Brochure]. Toronto, Canada: Author.

Morrison, K. T., Nelson, T. A., **M** & Ostry, A. S. (2011). **N** Methods for mapping local food production capacity from agricultural statistics. *Agricultural Systems,* **O** *104,* 491–499. **P** doi:10.1016/j .agsy.2011.03.006

Q Patent trials: Oracle, Google prepare for battle. (2012, April 12). **R** *Toronto Star,* **S** p. B4.

Include the DOI, if available, and in the format provided for both print and online sources

P

For an entry with no author or editor, move the title to the author position

Q

Capitalize and italicize the titles of periodicals (newspapers, journals, magazines)

R

Use "p." or "pp." for books, newspaper articles, and works in anthologies

S

General Formatting Rules

Formatting References list entries according to APA-style documentation rules requires **close attention to detail**.

The following rules provide the general guidelines. For examples of the most common sources that writers and students use as references, see *Section 6: References List Entries*.

ORDER OF REFERENCES

1 ALPHABETICAL ORDER

List entries alphabetically by the surname of the first author — here "Aucoin" before "MacLellan":

> Aucoin, P., Jarvis, M. D., & Turnbull, L. (2011). *Democratizing the Constitution: Reforming responsible government.* Toronto, Canada: Edmond Montgomery.

> MacLellan, L. (2012, February). In the company of strangers. *Report on Business, 28*(7), 14–16.

2 NO AUTHOR OR EDITOR

Move the title to the author position and list alphabetically by the first word of the title:

> Harvesting trees to make paper is bad. (n.d.). *Two sides.* Retrieved from http://www.twosides.us/harvesting-trees

> Patent trials: Oracle, Google prepare for battle. (2012, April 12). *Toronto Star,* p. B4.

3 NO AUTHOR, TITLE BEGINNING WITH "THE," "A," OR "AN"

List according to the first letter of the word immediately following "The," "A," or "An":

> The Doubleday Roget's thesaurus in dictionary form.

> An odyssey of Canadian verse.

4 MULTIPLE ENTRIES BY SAME AUTHOR

List by year of publication, earliest first:

> Freud, S. (1900).

> Freud, S. (1915).

5 SAME AUTHOR, SAME PUBLICATION DATE

Arrange alphabetically by title. Add the suffix (a, b, c, and so on) assigned to the year in both the References list and the in-text citation:

Frye, N. (1963a). *The educated imagination.*

Frye, N. (1963b). *Fables of identity.*

Frye, N. (1963c). *The well-tempered critic.*

6 DIFFERENT AUTHORS, SAME SURNAME

Arrange alphabetically by the first initial:

Hamilton, H.

Hamilton, J.

7 GROUP AUTHORS (ASSOCIATIONS, GOVERNMENT AGENCIES)

List by the first word of the name of the association:

Community Legal Education Ontario

Statistics Canada

CAPITALIZATION

1 TITLE OF AN ARTICLE, CHAPTER, OR WEB ARTICLE

Capitalize only the first letter of the title and any proper nouns:

Sibbald, B. (2012). Yes to ski helmets, but buyer beware [Editorial]. *Canadian Medical Association Journal, 184,* 627. doi:10.1503 /cmaj.120144

2 TITLE OF A NON-PERIODICAL (BOOK, BROCHURE, WEB DOCUMENT, AUDIOVISUAL PRODUCTION)

Capitalize only the first letter of the title and any proper nouns:

Farmers' markets get boost from province. (2008). *Orillia Farmers' Market.* Retrieved from http://www.orilliafarmersmarket.on.ca

Miller, S. (2008). *Edible action: Food activism & alternative economics.* Halifax, Canada: Fernwood.

3 PERIODICALS (NEWSPAPERS, JOURNALS, MAGAZINES, SCHOLARLY NEWSLETTERS)

Capitalize the title:

Schachter, H. (2012, May 13). Five major mistakes leaders make. *The Globe and Mail.* Retrieved from: http://theglobeandmail.com

4 WORD FOLLOWING A COLON

Capitalize the first letter and any proper nouns:

> Borderviews: Light plain/plane of light. (2012, March/April/May).
> *Border Crossings, 31*(1), 18.

5 IN-TEXT CITATION WITH TITLE IN PLACE OF AUTHOR

Capitalize the first letter of each word:

> A copyright trial with monumental implications for the technology
> industry is unfolding in a U.S. court. Oracle Corp. has charged that
> Google Inc. "stole its intellectual property to make Android software"
> ("Patent Trials," 2012, p. B4).

6 IN-TEXT REFERENCE TO TITLE OF ENTIRE WORK

Capitalize the first letter of each word:

> The movement towards consuming locally produced food received
> even greater attention and popularity with the publication of
> *The 100-Mile Diet: A Year of Local Eating* (2007) in which writers
> Smith and MacKinnon documented their year-long adventure with
> eating only food grown within a 100-mile radius of their apartment in
> Vancouver.

7 IN-TEXT REFERENCE TO TITLE OF AN ARTICLE OR CHAPTER

Capitalize the first letter of each word:

> In his report on the reopening of the Hamilton Farmers' Market,
> "Thinking Local, Acting Loco" (2011), Andrew Potter claimed that the
> rejection of numerous applications of previous long-term vendors such
> as Vietnamese and Middle Eastern food sellers was the result of the
> Market's "rebranding [and] pitching itself at the yuppie constituency"
> (p. 65).

ITALICS

1 TITLES OF PRINT, AUDIOVISUAL, AND ONLINE WORKS

Italicize the titles of books, journals, newspapers, magazines, reports, web documents, brochures, films, DVDs, and television and radio productions:

> Dery, L., & McCraw, K. (Producers), & Falaradeau, P. (Director).
>
> (2011). *Monsieur Lazhar* [Motion picture]. Canada: Micro_scope.

2 VOLUME NUMBER OF JOURNALS

Italicize the volume numbers:

> Corstjens, M., & Lal, R. (2012, April). Retail doesn't cross borders:
> Here's why and what to do about it. *Harvard Business Review*,
> *90*(4), 104–111.

3 IN-TEXT REFERENCES TO TITLES OF PRINT, AUDIOVISUAL, AND ONLINE WORKS

Italicize the titles of books, journals, newspapers, DVDs, and websites when referred to in-text:

> The movement towards consuming locally produced food received
> even greater attention and popularity with the publication of
> *The 100-Mile Diet: A Year of Local Eating* (2007), in which writers
> Smith and MacKinnon documented their year-long adventure with
> eating only food grown and produced within a 100-mile radius of their
> apartment in Vancouver.
>
> The *Orillia Farmers' Market* website lists key reasons to shop at
> farmers' markets, including the value of knowing where your food
> comes from, supporting family farmers, protecting the environment,
> and connecting with your community.

PARENTHESES

1 DATE OF PUBLICATION

Enclose the date of publication in parentheses:

> Community Legal Education Ontario. (2011). *A directory of
> community legal clinics in Ontario* [Brochure]. Toronto, Canada:
> Author.

2 JOURNAL ARTICLES WITH ISSUE NUMBERS

Enclose the issue number in parentheses immediately following the volume number for journals that begin each issue with page 1:

> Larch, M. (2006, September). Can we sustain sustainable agriculture? Learning from small-scale producer-suppliers in Canada and the U.K. *Geographical Journal, 172*(3), 230–244. http://dx.doi.org /10.1111/j.1475-4959.2006.00211.x

3 EDITORS

Enclose in parentheses the abbreviation "Ed." or "Eds." following the last editor's name:

> McBurney, M. (Ed.). (2012). *It's all about kindness: Remembering June Callwood*. Markham, Canada: Cormorant Books.

4 EDITIONS

Enclose the edition number and the abbreviation "ed." in parentheses:

> Guffey, M. E., Rhodes, K., & Rogin, P. (2011). *Business communication: Process and product* (6th Canadian ed.). Scarborough, Canada: Nelson.

5 SQUARE BRACKETS FOR NON-ROUTINE INFORMATION

Use square brackets immediately after the title and before the period to enclose non-routine information:

> Sibbald, B. (2012). Yes to ski helmets, but buyer beware [Editorial]. *Canadian Medical Association Journal, 184*, 627. doi:10.1503 /cmaj.120144

PAGINATION

1 ARTICLES OR CHAPTERS IN BOOKS, NEWSPAPERS, AND ANTHOLOGIES

Use "p." or "pp." to indicate the page numbers of book chapters and newspaper articles:

> Barata, P. (2012). Campaign against child poverty. In M. McBurney (Ed.), *It's all about kindness: Remembering June Callwood* (pp. 89–92). Markham, Canada: Cormorant Books.
>
> McCarthy, S., & Ibbitson, J. (2012, April 17). Why not try after-hours care the Dutch way? *The Globe and Mail*, pp. A1, A4.

2 ARTICLES IN MAGAZINES OR SCHOLARLY JOURNALS

Do not use "p." or "pp." to reference articles in magazines or scholarly journals:

> Potter, A. (2011, January 17). Thinking local, acting loco? *Maclean's*, *124*(1), 65–66.

> Townsend, A. R., Vitousek, P. M., & Houlton, B. Z. (2012). The climate benefits of better nitrogen and phosphorus management. *Issues in Science and Technology, 28*(2), 85–91.

DATE OF PUBLICATION

1 BOOKS AND SCHOLARLY JOURNALS

Include the year only in parentheses:

> Barata, P. (2012). Campaign against child poverty. In M. McBurney (Ed.), *It's all about kindness: Remembering June Callwood* (pp. 89–92). Markham, Canada: Cormorant Books.

2 NEWSPAPERS, JOURNALS, MAGAZINES, AND NEWSLETTERS

Use the following formats:

> Dailies and weeklies: (2012, June 1)

> Journals: (2011)

> Monthly magazines and newsletters: (2012, May)

> Bimonthly magazines and newsletters: (2012, January/February)

> Magazines and newsletters published seasonally or bi-annually: (2012, Summer)

> Work with no date available: (n.d.)

> Work accepted for publication but not yet printed: (in press)

PLACE OF PUBLICATION

Include the place of publication for **books, brochures, reports, and audio-visual productions**:

> Lawrence, G., Lyons, K. & Wallington, T. (2010). *Food security, nutrition and sustainability*. London, United Kingdom: Earthscan.

Do not include the place of publication or publisher's name for **newspapers, magazines, journals, and e-books**:

> Richler, J. (2010, September 20). A tale of two supermarkets. *Maclean's, 123*(36), 86.

> Smith, R. (2012). *Blindsided: How twenty years of writing about booze, drugs and sex ended in the blink of an eye.* Retrieved from http://www.kobobooks.com/

1 WORKS ORIGINATING IN THE UNITED STATES

List the place of publication as the city and state using the U.S. Postal Service abbreviation:

> Kandel, E. R. (2012). *The age of insight: The quest to understand the unconscious in art, mind, and brain, from Vienna 1900 to the present.* New York, NY: Random House.

2 WORKS ORIGINATING OUTSIDE THE UNITED STATES

List the place of publication as the city and country:

> Smith, A., & MacKinnon, J. B. (2007). *The 100-mile diet: A year of local eating.* Toronto, Canada: Random House.

APA does not specify whether or not to include provinces for Canadian references in materials published outside of the United States or for an international readership. Usage varies; please check with your instructor for their preference.

When two or more publisher locations are provided, use the location listed first.

PUBLISHER

Give the **name of the publisher** in as **brief** a form as possible. Omit terms such as Publishers, Co., or Inc., but include Press:

> Miller, S. (2008). *Edible action: Food activism & alternative economics.* Halifax, Canada: Fernwood.

> Wilson, D. A. (2011). *Thomas D'Arcy McGee: The extreme moderate, 1857–1868* (Vol. 2). Montreal, Canada: McGill-Queen's University Press.

6 References List Entries

"I never feel the soul of the plains express their quiet and peaceful beauty in a more inspiring way than when I stand on one of the bluffs of a river, looking out over the vast prairies at sunset time with the purple horizon as the background."

Jens Jensen, 1939

Jensen, J. (1990). *Siftings*. Baltimore, MD: Johns Hopkins University Press. (Original work published 1939)

Photo © Heather Holm

References List Entries

The following list provides examples of the most common sources that writers and students use as references.

The sample References list items will show you in what order to present **bibliographical information** (author, date, title, publisher) and when to use *italics*, CAPITALS, periods, spaces, etc., to format your entries.

If you use a reference source not listed here, refer to the latest edition of the *Publication Manual of the American Psychological Association*, *APA Style Guide to Electronic References*, and http://www.blog.apastyle.org.

ARTICLES IN BOOKS OR PERIODICALS

1   Article in a Magazine or Journal
2   Article in a Magazine or Journal (Two to Seven Authors)
3   Article in a Magazine or Journal (Eight or More Authors)
4   Article in a Magazine or Journal (No Author)
5   Article in a Magazine or Journal (Volume and Issue)
6   Article in a Magazine or Journal (Special Issue)
7   Article in a Newspaper
8   Article in a Newspaper (No Author)
9   Article/Chapter in an Edited Book or Anthology
10   Article/Chapter in a Multivolume Book
11   Editorial

12   Editorial (No Author)
13   Introduction/Foreword/Preface/Afterword
14   Letter to the Editor
15   Review of a Film, Performance, Book

BOOKS AND BROCHURES

16   Book by One Author
17   Book by Two or More Authors
18   Book by Translator
19   Book in Multiple Volumes
20   Book in Republished Edition
21   Book in Second and Subsequent Editions
22   Book with an Author and an Editor
23   Book/Textbook by Editor
24   Brochure
25   Brochure (No Date)
26   Classical Works
27   Government Document
28   Group or Corporate Author

ARTICLES IN BOOKS OR PERIODICALS

1 Article in a Magazine or Journal

MacLellan, L. (2012, February). In the company of strangers. *Report on Business, 28*(7), 14–16.

2 Article in a Magazine or Journal (Two to Seven Authors)

No DOI

Corstjens, M., & Lal, R. (2012, April). Retail doesn't cross borders: Here's why and what to do about it. *Harvard Business Review, 90*(4), 104–111.

With DOI

Iezzoni, L. I., & Ogg, M. (2012). Patient's perspective: Hard lessons from a long hospital stay. *American Journal of Nursing, 112*(4), 39–42. http://dx.doi.org/10.1097/01.NAJ.0000413457.53110.3a

For two to seven authors, include all names with commas between each and an ampersand (&) preceding the last name. If a print article has a DOI, include it in the reference entry as it appears in the document.

3 Article in a Magazine or Journal (Eight or More Authors)

Donnez, J., Tatarchuk, T. F., Bouchard, P., Puscasiu, L., Zakharenko, N. F., Ivanova, T., … Loumaye, E. (2012). UliPristal acetate versus placebo for fibroid treatment before surgery. *The New England Journal of Medicine, 366*, 409–419. doi:10.1056 /NEJMoa1103182

Include the first six authors, followed by ellipsis, then the last author.

4 Article in a Magazine or Journal (No Author)

Borderviews: Light plain/plane of light. (2012, March/April/May). *Border Crossings, 31*(1), 18.

Begin with the title of the article if there is no author.

5 Article in a Magazine or Journal (Volume and Issue)

Issues Individually Paged

Townsend, A. R., Vitousek, P. M., & Houlton, B. Z. (2012). The
climate benefits of better nitrogen and phosphorus management.
Issues in Science and Technology, 28(2), 85–91.

**Include the issue number in parentheses immediately
following the volume number with no space between for
journals that begin each issue with page 1.**

Issues Consecutively Paged

Morrow, R. L., Garland, E. J., Wright, J. M., Maclure, M., Taylor, S.,
& Dormuth, C. R. (2012). Influence of relative age on diagnosis
and treatment of attention-deficit/hyperactivity disorder in
children. *Canadian Medical Association Journal, 184*, 755–762.
doi:10.1503/cmaj.111619

**Do not include the issue number for journals with
consecutive paging issue to issue. Include the DOI if one is
assigned.**

6 Article in a Magazine or Journal (Special Issue)

Turner, M. (2011). Vancouver poetry in the early 1990s [Special
issue: Vancouver 125]. *subTerrain, 6*(59), 34–36.

**Use square brackets to include non-routine information such
as the title of a special issue or edition.**

7 Article in a Newspaper

Mason, G. (2012, February 12). Why not try after-hours care the
Dutch way? *The Globe and Mail*, p. A17.

McCarthy, S., & Ibbitson, J. (2012, April 17). Ottawa cuts
environmental role. *The Globe and Mail*, pp. A1, A4.

Picard, A. (2008, March 25). Recall issued for heparin marketed in
Canada. *The Globe and Mail*, p. A9.

**List all the pages separated by a comma for articles with
non-consecutive pages.**

8 Article in a Newspaper (No Author)

Patent trials: Oracle, Google prepare for battle. (2012, April 12).
Toronto Star, p. B4.

Place the title in the author position when no author is given.

9 Article/Chapter in an Edited Book or Anthology

Barata, P. (2012). Campaign against child poverty. In M. McBurney
(Ed.), *It's all about kindness: Remembering June Callwood*
(pp. 89–92). Markham, Canada: Cormorant Books.

Freud, S. (1995). The interpretation of dreams. In A. A. Brill (Ed.
& Trans.), *The basic writings of Sigmund Freud* (pp. 149–517).
New York, NY: Random House. (Original work published 1938)

10 Article/Chapter in a Multivolume Book

Wilson, D. A. (2011). A constitutional conservative: June 1863–
February 1864. In *Thomas D'Arcy McGee: The extreme moderate,
1857–1868* (Vol. 2, pp. 165–195). Montreal, Canada: McGill-
Queen's University Press.

11 Editorial

Sibbald, B. (2012). Yes to ski helmets, but buyer beware [Editorial].
Canadian Medical Association Journal, 184, 627. doi:10.1503
/cmaj.120144

The issues for this journal are paged consecutively from issue to issue; therefore, the issue number is not included here.

12 Editorial (No Author)

Steam engine time: Social networks are having their moment. How
long will it last? (2012). [Editorial]. *New Scientist, 213*(2852), 3.

Begin the entry with the title of the editorial when an editorial is unsigned (no author).

13 Introduction/Foreword/Preface/Afterword

Patwell, J. M. (2007). Introduction: Fundamentals of medical technology. In N. W. Dorland (Ed.), *Dorland's illustrated medical dictionary* (31st ed., pp. xxiii–xxvii). Philadelphia, PA: Saunders Elsevier.

14 Letter to the Editor

Craig, K. (2012, May). Penalty kick [Letter to the editor]. *The Walrus, 9*(4), 11.

15 Review of a Film, Performance, Book

Eatock, C. (2012, April 5). Out of the pit, into the spotlight [Review of the concert *National Ballet Orchestra 60th anniversary*]. *The Globe and Mail*, p. R4.

Ekers, M. (2012, April). Building forests [Review of the book *Eating dirt: Deep forests, big timber and life with the tree-planting tribe*, by C. Gill]. *Literary Review of Canada (LRC), 20*(3), 25.

Wheeler, B. (2012, May 18). The ballad of Saint Bob [Review of the film *Marley*, 2012]. *The Globe and Mail*, pp. R1, R3.

Use the reviewer's name as the author.
Add the release date after the title of a film, DVD, or other type of media.

BOOKS AND BROCHURES

16 Book by One Author

Kandel, E. R. (2012). *The age of insight: The quest to understand the unconscious in art, mind, and brain, from Vienna 1900 to the present*. New York, NY: Random House.

17 Book by Two or More Authors

Aucoin, P., Jarvis, M. D., & Turnbull, L. (2011). *Democratizing the Constitution: Reforming responsible government*. Toronto, Canada: Edmond Montgomery.

Include all authors to a maximum of seven. For eight or more, include the first six authors, followed by ellipsis, then the last author.

18 Book by Translator

Leroux, G. (2010). *Partita for Glenn Gould: An inquiry into the nature of genius* (D. Winkler, Trans.). Montreal, Canada: McGill-Queen's University Press. (Original work published 2007)

19 Book in Multiple Volumes

Wilson, D. A. (2011). *Thomas D'Arcy McGee: The extreme moderate, 1857–1868* (Vol. 2). Montreal, Canada: McGill-Queen's University Press.

20 Book in Republished Edition

Agamben, G. (2007). *The coming community* (M. Hardt, Trans.). Minneapolis, MN: University of Minnesota Press. (Original work published 1993)

21 Book in Second and Subsequent Editions

Guffey, M. E., Rhodes, K., & Rogin, P. (2011). *Business communication: Process and product* (6th Canadian ed.). Scarborough, Canada: Nelson.

22 Book with an Author and an Editor

Shelley, M. (2000). *Frankenstein* (2nd ed., J. M. Smith, Ed.). Boston, MA: Bedford-St. Martin's. (Original work published 1818)

For classic texts or older works, cite the original date of publication following the standard reference entry as in the example above.

23 Book/Textbook by Editor

McBurney, M. (Ed.). (2012). *It's all about kindness: Remembering June Callwood*. Markham, Canada: Cormorant Books.

24 Brochure

Community Legal Education Ontario. (2011). *A directory of community legal clinics in Ontario* [Brochure]. Toronto, Canada: Author.

25 Brochure (No Date)

Lake Simcoe Region Conservation Authority. (n.d.). *LEAP (Landowner environmental assistance program)* [Brochure]. Newmarket, Canada: Author.

Ontario Ministry of Health. (n.d.). *Learn where you can go for health care in your community* [Brochure]. Toronto, Canada: Author.

Use (n.d.) if no date is available.
When the author is a group or corporation, the publisher is often the same organization. In this instance, use Author as the publisher.

26 Classical Works

Classical works such as ancient Greek works and the Bible are not listed in your References list. Refer to them by part in the text of your paper (e.g., chapters, verses, lines) and identify the version in the first citation, for example, 1 Cor. 13:1–13 (New Revised Standard Version). See **Section 4: Using In-Text Citations**, *Parts of Classic Works*.

27 Government Document

Statistics Canada. (2010). *Human activity and the environment: Freshwater supply and demand in Canada, 2010.* (16-201-XPE). Ottawa, Canada: Ministry of Industry.

28 Group or Corporate Author

Canadian Auto Workers. (2012). *Re-thinking Canada's auto industry: A policy vision to escape the race to the bottom.* Toronto, Canada: Author.

OTHER PUBLICATIONS

29 Comic Strip

Harrop, G. (2012, May 10). Backbench: MP's – off the record [Comic strip]. *The Globe and Mail*, p. R6.

30 Entry in an Atlas

Ballard, R. D. (2001). A Titanic explorer. In S. A. Earle, *Atlas of the ocean: The deep frontier* (pp. 64–73). Washington, DC: National Geographic.

Bertaux, J. L. (1996). Comets. In J. Audouze & G. Israel (Eds.), *The Cambridge atlas of astronomy* (3rd ed., pp. 234–237). Cambridge, United Kingdom: Cambridge University Press.

31 Map

Simcoe County Farm Fresh Marketing Association. (2010). *Buy fresh buy local: Your year-round guide to buying local food* [Map]. Barrie, Canada: Author.

32 Encyclopedia/Dictionary

Ayto, J. (2006). *Brewer's dictionary of phrase and fable* (17th ed.). New York, NY: HarperCollins.

Murray, J. A. H. et al. (Eds.). (1989). *The Oxford English dictionary* (2nd ed., Vol. 1–20). Oxford, United Kingdom: Oxford University Press.

Tanton, J. S. (2005). *Encyclopedia of mathematics*. New York, NY: Facts on File.

List the name of the lead editor only, as in the Murray example, followed by "et al." for a major reference work with a large editorial board.

33 Entry in an Encyclopedia/Dictionary

Green, K. P. (2010). Carbon taxes. In S. I. Dutch (Ed.), *Encyclopedia of global warming* (Vol. 1, pp. 181–182). Pasadena, CA: Salem Press.

Pratt, R. (1999). Phoenix. In *Encyclopedia of Greek mythology* (Vol. 3, pp. 521–522). Oxford, United Kingdom: Oxford University Press.

34 Entry in an Encyclopedia/Dictionary (No Author)

Doppler effect. (2002). In P. Moore (Ed.), *Astronomy encyclopedia: An A–Z guide to the universe* (p. 117). New York, NY: Oxford University Press.

Hypercalcemic nephropathy. (2009). *Mosby's dictionary of medicine, nursing & health professions* (8th ed., p. 906). St. Louis, MO: Elsevier Health Sciences.

Place the title of the entry in the author position when no author is provided.

35 Media Release

Natural Resources Canada. (2012, January 9). *An open letter from the Honourable Joe Oliver, Minister of Natural Resources, on Canada's commitment to diversify our energy markets and the need to further streamline the regulatory process in order to advance Canada's national economic interest* [Media release].

36 Unpublished Paper Presented in a Meeting

Vardalos, M. (2008, May). *Terrorized by melancholy: The science of depression and the production of the happy consciousness.* Paper presented at The Human Condition Series Conference, Georgian College, Barrie, Canada.

37 Film

Dery, L., & McCraw, K. (Producers), & Falaradeau, P. (Director). (2011). *Monsieur Lazhar* [Motion picture]. Canada: Micro_scope.

Place the producer in the author position, followed by the director. The date refers to the release date of the film; the country is the country of origin. The production studio is in the publisher position.

38 DVD

Bozzo, S. (Producer/Director). (2008). *Blue gold: World water wars* [DVD]. United States: Purple Turtle Films.

39 Television Broadcast

McKeon, R. (Writer), Guerriero, L., & Softly, P. (Producers/Directors). (2012). The wreck of the Costa Concordia [Television series episode]. In J. Williamson (Executive Producer), *The fifth estate*. Toronto, Canada: CBC.

Use the same format as a chapter in a book for a single episode in a series. See entry 9. Place the writer/script writer in the author position followed by the director. Add the producer/executive producer in the editor position. Identify roles in parentheses following the names.

40 Music Recording/CD

Lennon, J., & McCartney, P. (1965). In my life. On *Rubber soul* [Record]. London, United Kingdom: Capitol.

Locke, M. (2001). Suite No. 1 in G minor-major. [Recorded by T. Haig, E. Soderstrom, & O. Fortin]. On *Matthew Locke: Consorts in two parts* [CD]. New York, NY: Dorian Recordings. (Original work published 1672)

Place the writer in the author position followed by the copyright year and the title of the musical piece. The artist's name is next if different from the writer. The title of the complete work and the medium, identified in brackets, follow. The label is in the publisher position.

41 Work of Art

Andrews, S. (2008). *Crowd* [Painting]. *Canadian Art, 24*(4), 40.

Harris, L. S. (1917). *Snow* [Painting]. McMichael Canadian Art Collection, Kleinburg, Canada.

Include the source of the reproduction in your entry, as in the first example, to reference a photograph of a work.

Name the gallery or institution that houses an original work in order to reference it.

ELECTRONIC SOURCES

ONLINE WEB PAGES, ARTICLES, AND DOCUMENTS

Include a reference and in-text citation when a particular article or web page is discussed.

42 Article with a DOI

Kaplan, A. A. (2012). 54-year-old man with a chronic cough— A primary care perspective from Canada. *Primary Care Respiratory Journal, 21*(3), 342–343. http://dx.doi.org/10.4101 /pcrj.2012.00075

43 Article from a Website (No DOI)

On sludge: Policy on applying biosolids on farmland. (2010). *Ecological Farmers of Ontario*. Retrieved from http://www.efao .ca/index.cfm?pagePath=Policies_Issues/On_Sludge&id=26946

Wood, J. (2012). *Canadian environmental indicators — air quality*. Retrieved from http://www.fraserinstitute.org/uploadedFiles /fraser-ca/Content/research-news/research/publications/canadian -environmental-indicators-air-quality-2012.pdf

44 Article from a Website (No Date)

Colosi, J. A., & Lynch, J. F. (n.d.). *Some thoughts on the outstanding acoustical and oceanographic issues concerning "solibore" internal waves*. Retrieved from http://www.whoi.edu /science/AOPE/people/tduda/isww/text/colosi/colosi.htm

Didier, S. (n.d.). What does sustainable food mean? *National Geographic*. Retrieved from http://greenliving .nationalgeographic.com/sustainable-food-mean-2944.html

45 Article from a Website (No Author, No Date, No DOI)

Harvesting trees to make paper is bad. (n.d.). *Two sides*. Retrieved from http://www.twosides.us/harvesting-trees

Move the web page's title to the author position when no author is identified.

46 Article from a Database (With DOI)

Iezzoni, L. I., & Ogg, M. (2012). Patient's perspective: Hard lessons from a long hospital stay. *American Journal of Nursing, 112*(4), 39–42. http://dx.doi.org/10.1097/01.NAJ.0000413457.53110.3a

Vallerand, R. J. (2012). From motivation to passion: In search of the motivational processes involved in a meaningful life. *Canadian Psychology*, 53(1), 42–52. doi:10.1037/a0026377

Include the DOI, if available, as it appears in the document.

47 Article Retrieved Online or from a Database (No DOI)

Cyboran, S. F., & Goldsmith, C. (2012). Making the case: New study shows it does, indeed, pay to become a healthy enterprise. *Benefits Quarterly*, 28(1), 26–37. Retrieved from http://www.sibson.com/publications-and-resources/articles/ISCEBS-Benefits-Quarterly.pdf

If an article with no DOI is found in a database, a web search is required to find either the direct link (full URL) or the journal/magazine/newspaper/publisher's home page URL. Use the direct link or home page URL, whichever is more dependable, in your retrieval statement.

48 Article Available ONLY in a Database (No DOI)

Thompson, K. J., Thach, E. C., & Morelli, M. (2010). Implementing ethical leadership: Current challenges and solutions. *Insights to a Changing World Journal*, (4), 107–130. Retrieved from http://www.ebscohost.com/academic/academic-search-complete

Thompson, K. J., Thach, E. C., & Morelli, M. (2010). Implementing ethical leadership: Current challenges and solutions. *Insights to a Changing World Journal*, (4), 107–130. Retrieved from http://www.franklinpublishing.net/insightstoachangingworld.html

In the retrieval statement include the most reliable method of retrieval from the following options: the journal's home page URL, the database home page URL, or the database name and accession number (no URL).

49 Thesis Retrieved from a Database (No DOI)

Statham, T. R. (2011). *Dogma and history in Victorian Scotland*.
(Doctoral dissertation). Retrieved from ProQuest Dissertations
and Theses. (AAT NR74796)

**Include the database name in the retrieval statement
followed by the accession or order number if one is
assigned.**

50 Article in an Internet-Only Magazine or Journal (With DOI)

Roze, D. (2012). Disentangling the benefits of sex. *PLoS Biology,
10*(5). doi:10.1371/journal.pbio,1001317

Some online journals do not provide page numbers.

51 Article in an Internet-Only Magazine or Journal (No Author, No DOI)

Environment chief backs gas 'fracking' and nuclear in the UK. (2012,
May 8). *Ecologist*. Retrieved from http://www.theecologist.org
/News/news_analysis/1361478/environment_chief_backs_gas
_fracking_and_nuclear_in_the_uk.html

52 Document Available on College/University Program or Department Website (No Author, No Date)

Athabasca University. (n.d.). *The AU library guide to the research
process*. Retrieved from http://library.athabascau.ca/help/guide
/guide2research.html

53 Government Document

Canadian Museum of Nature. (2011). *They came from far and wide
... 2010–2011 annual report*. Retrieved from http://nature.ca
/sites/default/files/docs/ann10-11nature_e.pdf

Statistics Canada. (2012). *Highlights and analyses of the 2011
census of agriculture*. Retrieved from http://www.statcan.gc.ca
/pub/95-640-x/2012002/05-eng.htm

54 Annual Corporate Report

Bombardier. (2010). *Turning obstacles into opportunity: Bombardier annual report year ended January 31, 2010.* Retrieved from http://www2.bombardier.com/en/7_0/pdf/annual _report_2010.pdf

55 Curriculum Guide

Manitoba Education. (2011). *Grade 12 current topics in First Nations, Metis, and Inuit studies: A foundation for implementation.* Retrieved from http://www.edu.gov.mb.ca/k12 /abedu/foundation_gr12/full_doc.pdf

56 Newspaper Article

Schachter, H. (2012, May 13). Five major mistakes leaders make. *The Globe and Mail.* Retrieved from http://www.theglobeandmail .com

57 Newspaper Article (No Author)

Investing in education crucial. (2012, March 16). *Toronto Star.* Retrieved from http://www.thestar.com

58 Review of a Film, Performance, Book

Pardy, B. (2012, March). A right to clean air? Constitutional protection for the environment may leave people out of luck [Review of the book *The environmental rights revolution: A global study of constitutions, human rights and the environment,* by D. R. Boyd]. *Literary Review of Canada (LRC).* Retrieved from http://reviewcanada.ca/reviews/2012/03/01 /a-right-to-clean-air/

Use the reviewer's name as the author.

59 Media Release

Government of Canada. (2012, March 14). *PM launches Vimy Foundation Pin Campaign* [Media release]. Retrieved from http://www.pm.gc.ca/eng/media.asp?category=1&featureId =6&pageId=26&id=4688

60 Online Brochure

Community Legal Education Ontario. (2012). *Rent increases* [Brochure]. Retrieved from http://www.cleo.on.ca/english/pub /onpub/PDF/landlordTenant/rentincs.pdf

61 Online Map

Simcoe County Farm Fresh Marketing Association. (2010). *Buy fresh buy local: Your year-round guide to buying local food* [Map]. Retrieved from http://www.simcoecountyfarmfresh.ca /route.php

62 Image from a Website

Hiking trail in the forest. (2012). *Canadian Forest Service.* Retrieved from http://cfs.nrcan.gc.ca/pages/121

Zufelt, K. (2012). *Boreal chickadee.* Retrieved from http://cfs.nrcan .gc.ca/pages/254

The image's title can often be found by putting a cursor over the image.

Use the image's title as author when no photo credit is provided.

ONLINE ENCYCLOPEDIAS/DICTIONARIES, BOOKS, WIKIS

63 Entry in an Encyclopedia or Dictionary

Anilniliak, N. (2012). Ukkusiksalik National Park. In *The Canadian encyclopedia: Historica Foundation of Canada.* Retrieved from http://www.thecanadianencyclopedia.com

Venes, D. (n.d.). Diabetes. Taber's Cyclopedic Medical Dictionary

(21st ed.) [Mobile application software]. Retrieved from http://

www.skyscape.com/estore/ProductDetail.aspx?ProductId=2509

For handheld applications (apps) include the version, if available (Version 2.01), and [Mobile application software] immediately following the title and before the period.

Titles of software and apps are not italicized.

The retrieval statement should provide the home/search page where the app can be downloaded.

64 Entry in an Encyclopedia or Dictionary (No Author)

Hegemony. (n.d.). In *Merriam-Webster's online dictionary*.

Retrieved from http://www.merriam-webster.com/dictionary

/hegemony

Place the title of the entry in the author position when no author is provided.

65 Entry in an Encyclopedia or Dictionary (With Editor)

Lindemans, M. F. (Ed.). (2002). Asgard. In *Encyclopedia mythica*.

Retrieved from http://www.pantheon.org/articles/a/asgard.html

66 Wiki

Aggression. (2010, November 24). Retrieved May 15, 2012, from

http://psychwiki.com/wiki/Aggression

Wikis are web pages with ever-changing content where public users contribute to and edit the articles. Since the authorship is collaborative, and therefore unknown, insert the title of the article as author.

Provide a retrieval date when the website is likely updated or changed frequently, for example, with Wikis and social network pages.

67 E-Book

Thoreau, H. D. (2011). *On the duty of civil disobedience*. Retrieved from http://www.gutenberg.org/files/71/71-h/71-h.htm (Original work published 1849)

68 E-Book for Purchase Online

Nelson, G. C. (2011). *Food security, farming, and climate change to 2050: Scenarios, results, policy options* [iBook 1.3.1 version]. Retrieved from http://www.apple.com/itunes/whats-on/

Smith, R. (2012). *Blindsided: How twenty years of writing about booze, drugs and sex ended in the blink of an eye*. Retrieved from http://www.kobobooks.com/

Provide the home page only if the URL is long. Include the electronic reader version if applicable.

69 E-Book from a Database (No DOI)

Polette, N. (2010). *Reading the world with picture books.* Retrieved from http://www.ebscohost.com/ebooks

70 E-Book or Research Report with Corporate Author

Automotive Industry Association of Canada. (2010). *2010 Canadian automotive service & repair shop survey: Benchmarking performance*. Retrieved from http://www.aiacanada.com /uploads/2010_website/publications/2010_Automotive_Shop _Survey_en_March_16_2010_V2.pdf

Tourism Industry Association of Canada, Parks Canada, & Canadian Tourism Commission. (2008). *Green your business toolkit*. Retrieved from http://www.tiac.travel/documents/advocacy /green_your_business_toolkit.pdf

71 Chapter in an E-Book (With DOI)

Kroll, J. F., Dussias, P. E., Bogulski, C. A., & Kroff, J. R. V. (Eds.).
(2012). Juggling two languages in one mind: What bilinguals tell
us about language processing and its consequences for cognition.
In *The psychology of learning and motivation* (Vol. 56,
pp. 229–262). doi:10.1016/B978-0-12-394393-4.00007-8

BLOGS AND PODCASTS

A blog is a web log.

Use the author's name, screen name (as posted), or both if available.

Do not use italics for the title, subject, or thread for blog posts.

Use italics for the title of podcasts. Identify the type of posting in square brackets following the title.

In the retrieval statement, give the URL where the message can be retrieved.

72 Blog Post

Trail, G. (2012, May 15). Constructing lunch [Blog post]. Retrieved
from: http://www.yougrowgirl.com/category/grow/

73 Blog Post Comment

Freemantle, P. (2012, April 14). Re: Allowed harvest levels on
Haida Gwaii cut in half [Blog comment]. Retrieved from http://
foresttalk.com/index.php/2012/04/05/allowed-harvest-levels-on
-haida-gwaii-cut-in-half/#comments

Provide the screen name as well as the real name, when available, in Blogs and Twitter postings. See examples #74 and #79.

74 Video Blog Post

Vsauce Michael. (2012, May 12). *Why is yawning contagious?* [Video blog post]. Retrieved from http://www.youtube.com /watch?v=jGIbUK4nw00

Provide the screen name as posted.

Italicize the titles of video blog posts since they are commonly stand alone documents.

75 Audio Podcast

Brooks, T. (2012). *Radiation exposure: The long view* [Audio podcast]. Retrieved from http://www.nature.com/nature/podcast/

76 Television/Film/Visual Podcast

CBC Digital Archives. (2012). *Emily Carr: Artist, author, eccentric* [Television broadcast]. Retrieved from http://www.cbc.ca /archives/categories/arts-entertainment/visual-arts/visual-arts -general/emily-carr-artist-author-eccentric.html

Use the director or producer of a film as the author.

In square brackets, identify the type of production: Motion picture, Documentary, Interview, Television broadcast, Audio podcast, or Video blog post (e.g., YouTube).

SOCIAL NETWORKS

When discussing a website in general, the URL is included in-text, but not in the References list. However, when a specific post is discussed, both an in-text citation as well as a References list entry are required.

77 Facebook — Page or Note

Canadian Red Cross. (2012, November 9). One day on earth 11.11.11 [Facebook note]. Retrieved November 19, 2012 from https://www.facebook.com/canadianredcross

Include a retrieval date for web page URLs that are likely to be updated and changed, such as social networking pages and Wikis.

Provide the type of page in square brackets for publicly available pages from Facebook.

78 Facebook — Private Pages

Treat online private pages the same as personal communications since the accessibility is limited and often restricted.

Provide the URL of the site in text and not in the References list.

79 Twitter

Harper, S. [Stephen]. (2012, March 14). Launched the Vimy Foundation Pin Campaign to raise awareness of the Battle of Vimy Ridge. Lest we forget: http://ow.ly/9F9KK [Tweet]. Retrieved from https://twitter.com/#!/pmharper

Provide the screen name as posted in square brackets following the user's real name, if known.

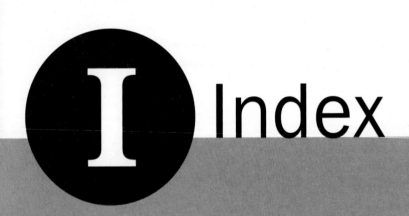

Index

Index

Index

Index

Index